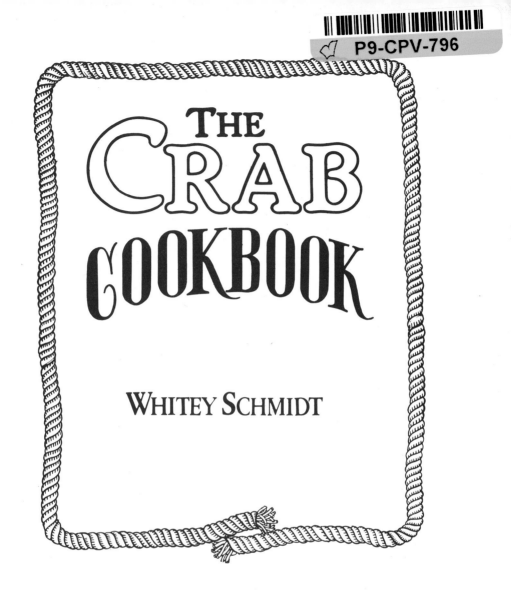

THE CRAB COOKBOOK

WHITEY SCHMIDT

MARIAN HARTNETT PRESS

Printed in the
United States of America
First Printing 1990
ISBN 0-9613008-8-4

Library of Congress Catalog Number 89-81335
Copyright 1990 by Marian Hartnett Press
Box 88
Crisfield, Maryland 21817

CONTENTS

CONTENTS

INTRODUCTION

The Crab Cookbook began when I first started collecting crab recipes about 25 years ago. Many recipes were gathered during trips around the Chesapeake Bay; others came from trips along the east coast from the Florida Keys to Nova Scotia and on the west coast from Mexico to Vancouver. I met some of the country's best cooks. I saved their recipes, stuffing what I could into loose-leaf notebooks. I have scribbled on placemats in restaurants and jammed them into my cookbook collection. Many have been clipped from local newspapers and magazines. Some are family favorites handed down from generation to generation, some are old, and some are new recipes, but all are examples of true crab country cookery. All have been home tested, some many times. I've tried to duplicate the dishes without sacrificing authenticity of either taste or appearance. This is a personal collection of recipes that have passed the "taste test."

A special thanks goes to those who have conveyed their recipes to me in their enthusiasm for crab cookery.

Illustrations by
Margaret Scott

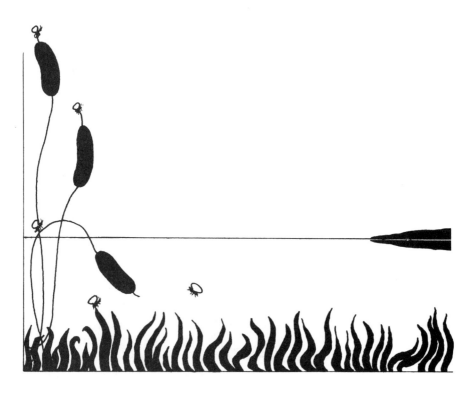

Crab Cookery

MEET THE BLUE CRAB

The meat from all varieties of crabs—blue, Dungeness, king, and stone—can be used interchangeably in the recipes in this cookbook. With this book as your guide, you will be able to enjoy crab dishes as often as you like, and let it add a healthy, delicious, and new dimension to your meal planning.

Crab meat is an excellent source of high quality protein, vitamins, and minerals that are needed for good nutrition. Per 3½-ounce serving, a blue or soft crab has 81 calories with 80-100 mgs. cholesterol, a Dungeness crab has 87 calories with 60 mgs. cholesterol, and a king crab has 74 calories with 60 mgs. cholesterol.*

The most popular crab, the blue crab, supplies almost 75 percent of the crabs marketed in the United States. Despite its fearsome appearance and aggressive nature, the blue crab is a greatly cherished seafood. Many gourmets prefer the blue crab's sweet meat over all other seafood.

Crab cookery offers endless opportunities for exploration and delight whether it be appetizers, soups, salads, crab cakes, soft shell crabs, deviled crab, or crab imperial.

Crabs are sometimes called: buckram, buffalo, buster, buster sook, blue, Jimmy, Jimmy Dick, Jimmy chandler, orange crab, sponge crab, sook, Sally, peeler, and soft as well as delicious, tasty, savory, zesty, mouth-watering, and delectable.

✳ *The Great American Seafood Cookbook* by Susan Hermann Loomis. (Workman Publishing. New York).

IN THE MARKETPLACE

Step up to the seafood counter and you will see an enticing display of one type of blue crab meat or another. How do you choose? Fresh picked blue crab meat is divided into three separate categories of different quality.

Lump Meat or **Backfin:** This is solid lumps of white meat picked from the backfin section of the crab. It is the most expensive meat picked, and the large nuggets are used in recipes where appearance is important.

Special (regular): It is small white flakes of meat from the body of the crab.

Claw Meat: It's picked from the claws and is quite dark and rich in flavor. Claw meat is used in recipes where appearance is not important and is generally lower priced than the preceding grades.

Cocktail crab claws: These are sold at the seafood counter in cans labeled fresh or fresh pasteurized. Cocktail claws are the last segment of the claw. The shell has been completely removed, except for the tip, which may serve as a handle for dipping meat in cocktail sauce. They may also be called crab fingers or cocktail delight.

A similar product in the frozen food case contains the claw of snow crabs, a species with larger claws.

CATEGORIZING THE CRAB

DUNGENESS CRAB: It is two to three times larger than the blue crab. Fresh cooked meat is picked from both body and claws and packed as one grade. It has a pinkish tinge. It comes from the Pacific coast and weighs in at 1¾ pounds to 3½ pounds. Market forms are live, cooked in the shell, fresh cooked meat, frozen cooked meat, and canned cooked meat.

KING CRAB: It is sold as legs or claws in the shell as well as frozen or previously frozen. King crab legs come from the north Pacific off the Alaska coast. Big ones measure 6 feet from the tip of one leg to the tip of the opposite leg.

STONE CRAB: The stone crab is harvested along the Florida coast, and only the claws are marketed. They are cooked immediately on landing and are sold cooked. Most people are purists when it comes to stone crab and prefer it cold or steamed only long enough to heat it. Carefully use a heavy-duty nut cracker or hammer to crack the claws. Serve with a tasty mustard sauce.

HOW TO COOK CRABS

STEAMED CRABS

1 dozen live crabs

1 cup vinegar

1 cup beer

3 tablespoons salt

3 tablespoons seafood seasoning

Pot should have a raised rack, minimum 2 inches high. Add equal quantities of vinegar and beer to just below level of rack. Layer crabs; sprinkle each layer with mixture of seafood seasoning and salt. Cover and steam until crabs are red.

BOILED CRABS

Boil enough heavily-salted water to cover however many crabs you have. Add live crabs quickly and bring back to a boil. Cook 10 minutes and drain. You may wish to spice your crabs by adding the following ingredients to the salted water.

1 lemon cut in half

6 bay leaves

freshly-ground pepper

2 teaspoons vinegar

2 cloves of garlic, mashed

HOW TO PICK A CRAB

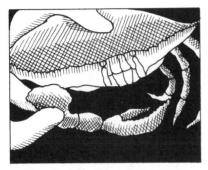

1. Break off claws.

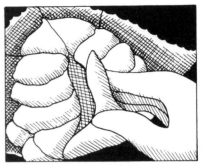

2. Lift apron.

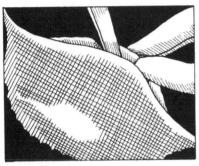

3. Pry up top shell.

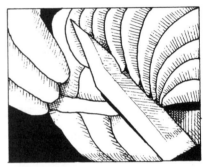

4. Scrape off feathery gills.

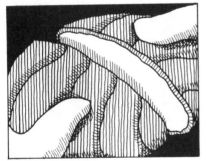

5. Break apart at center.

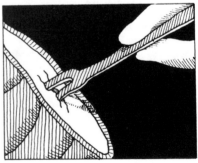

6. Pick out the meat.

"Don't Smash 'em,
Just Crack 'em"

IN-THE-SAUCE

Sauces and spices add extra magic to crab cookery. Cooked crab meat tastes great just as it is, but it is also delicious when enhanced with other flavors. A few items you can use to add zest to your crab dishes are lemon and garlic butter, fresh diced ginger and soy sauce, vinegar and seafood seasoning, ketchup and horseradish, white wine and tarragon vinegar, and garlic-soy dipping sauce. Following is one of my favorite dipping sauces.

MUSTARD SAUCE

This recipe originated at Joe's Stone Crab Restaurant in Miami. It's a classic when serving up sea-fresh, scrumptious crabs. You can visit Joe's or steam the crabs yourself, but be sure to give it a try.

Put the English mustard in a sauce pan, then add the mayonnaise and heat for one minute. Add the remaining ingredients and beat until the mixture reaches a creamy consistency. Chill. Serves 4.

3½ teaspoons Coleman's Dry English Mustard
1 cup mayonnaise
2 teaspoons Worcestershire sauce
1 teaspoon A-1 Sauce
⅛ cup light cream
⅛ teaspoon salt

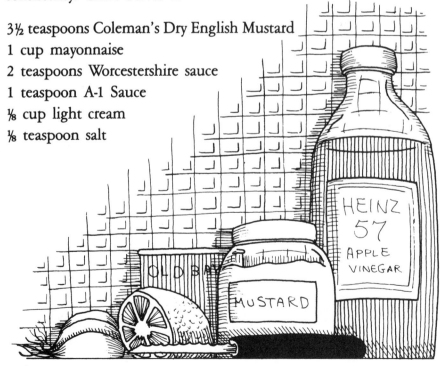

PUTTING THE BITE ON SOFT SHELL CRABS

Soft shell crabs are an east coast tradition. The crab in its soft stage is not harvested out west. The soft crab industry began during the 1870's in Crisfield, Maryland and today, the soft shell crab represents a major Chesapeake Bay commercial effort.

In order for a blue crab to increase in size, the crab must first molt or shed its hard shell. Under the hard shell is a new, soft shell. The delectable soft shell crab must be caught right after it has molted. If left in the water, its shell will begin to harden in about two hours. Soft shell crabs are available from late spring to early fall with May through August the most productive months.

As the availability of crabs increases during the summer, prices will drop. You may wish to purchase a quantity of them when the price is low and keep them for future use. They should be cleaned and individually wrapped before storing them in the freezer. This can be easily accomplished by wrapping the cleaned crab with its legs folded under its body.

Some methods for preparing soft shells are baked, sautéed, deep fat fried or pan fried. Other ways of cooking will give equally tasty results. Soft shell crab sandwiches are one of life's greatest pleasures. Soft crabs are marked in the following manner and are sold live, fresh dressed or frozen.

Medium	2.5 to 4.0 inches
Hotel	4.0 to 4.5 inches
Prime	4.5 to 5.0 inches
Jumbo	5.0 to 5.5 inches
Whale	over 5.5 inches

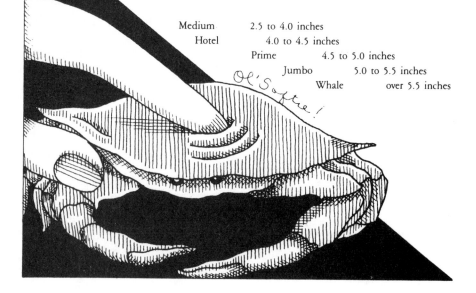

Ol' Softie!

HOW TO DRESS SOFT SHELL CRABS

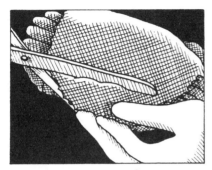

1. Cut crab across face.

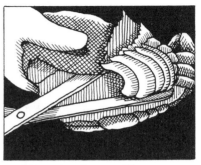

2. Trim feathery gills.

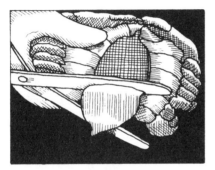

3. Cut off apron.

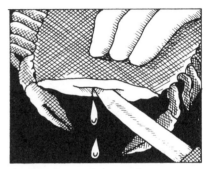

4. Drain well, pat dry.

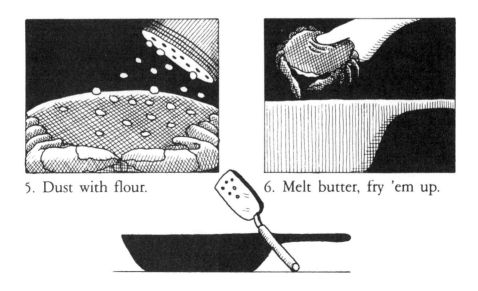

5. Dust with flour.

6. Melt butter, fry 'em up.

CRABETTES

Stone crab meat is so rich, purchase only three large claws per person.

Pasteurized crab meat is fresh crab meat that has been heated and vacuum-sealed to keep longer.

The bigger the crab, the bigger the price.

The secret to good crab picking is a good crab knife.

Save your crab shells. This Neptune China makes unique dishes for crab imperial or deviled crab. Scrub the shells with a brush until clean, cover with hot water in a pot, and add 1 teaspoon of baking soda. Bring the water to a boil, lower the heat, and let simmer for 20 minutes.

If he ain't kickin', he ain't cookin'.

Allow at least six steamed crabs per person when serving steamed crab.

When buying soft shell crabs, buy two for each person.

One pound of cooked crab meat is usually sufficient for most dishes that serve four persons.

Soft crabs are most plentiful when the moon is full.

Hard crabs have more meat in them when the moon is on the wane.

To keep soft shell crabs from popping when frying, puncture the legs and claws with a sharp fork.

The peak of the soft shell crab season is during the summer months in May to August.

Crab meat is shelled by hand and it's hard to remove the meat without taking some shell with it. That's why you may find tiny pieces of shell in canned crab meat. Sometimes you will also find tiny yellow or orange lumps in crab meat. These are pieces of edible fat.

Appetizers

PENINSULA CRAB DABS

1 pound crab meat
⅓ cup fine soft bread crumbs
2 tablespoons dry sherry
1 teaspoon chopped chives
1 teaspoon dry mustard
¼ teaspoon salt
10 slices bacon, cut in thirds
4 tablespoons mayonnaise

Remove cartilage from crab meat. Combine all ingredients except bacon. Mix thoroughly. Chill for 30 minutes. Portion crab mixture with a tablespoon. Shape into small rolls. Wrap bacon around crab rolls and secure with a toothpick. Place crab rolls on a broiler pan. Broil about 4 inches from source of heat for 8 to 10 minutes or until bacon is crisp. Turn carefully. Broil 4 to 5 minutes longer. Makes 30 hors d'oeuvres.

This dish is not only easy, it's fun to serve. When the bacon is cooked, transfer to a serving platter and serve warm.

Crab Collection

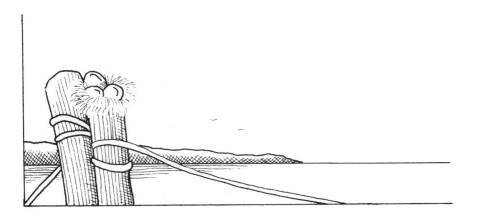

MATT'S CRAB MEAT BITES

½ pound crab meat
½ cup butter, softened
1 (5-ounce) jar sharp pasteurized process cheese spread
¼ teaspoon garlic salt
¼ teaspoon seasoned salt
1½ teaspoons mayonnaise
1 (12-ounce) package English muffins

Combine first six ingredients, blending well. Chill. Split muffins in half; spread with cheese mixture. Cut each muffin half into quarters. Broil until puffed and golden. Yield: 4 dozen.

This recipe is easy to prepare. The hard part is keeping the serving platter well stocked.

Matt Schmidt, Clinton, Maryland

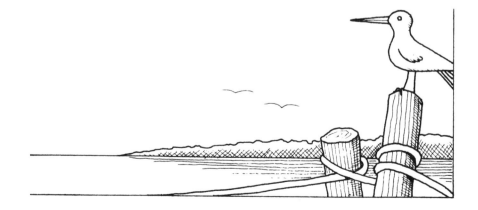

CRAB REGAL

1/2 pound backfin crab meat

¼ cup plain, lowfat yogurt

3 tablespoons catsup

¼ tablespoon lemon juice

1 teaspoon Worcestershire sauce

⅛ teaspoon salt

dash white pepper

⅛ teaspoon seafood seasoning

2 tablespoons fresh parsley, chopped

¼ tablespoon seasoned bread crumbs

4 strips bacon, cut into 1-inch pieces

Pack crab meat into 40 cleaned little neck clam shells. In a small bowl, mix together the next seven ingredients. Spoon about ⅔ teaspoon of sauce over each hors d'oeuvre, covering all crab meat. Sprinkle each with parsley and bread crumbs. Top with bacon. Place under preheated broiler and broil until bacon is crisp. Yields 40 Servings.

This excellent recipe is adapted from the Maryland Seafood Cookbook. It gets added zest when topped with bacon. Enjoy.

Crab Collection

CRAB MEAT PARTY APPETIZERS

8-ounce package cream cheese, softened
6 ounces crab meat
¼ cup green onion slices
1 garlic clove, minced
6 egg roll wrappers, cut into quarters
1 egg, beaten
sweet and sour sauce

Combine cream cheese, crab meat, onions and garlic; mix well. Spoon 1 tablespoon cream cheese mixture onto center of each egg roll quarter. Brush edges of each quarter with egg. Bring opposite corners of each quarter to center; twist top. Press edges to seal. Fry 2 minutes in deep hot oil (375 degrees), or until golden brown, turning over. Drain on paper towels. Serve with sweet and sour sauce, if desired. Makes 2 dozen.

Home entertaining can and should be a very personal thing. Planning is the key to successful entertaining. Pick a theme along with appropriate food and a complementary color scheme.

Capital Newspaper, Annapolis, Maryland

CHEEZY CRAB HORS D'OEUVRE

1 8-ounce package cream cheese, softened
1 tablespoon milk
1 cup Maryland crab meat
2 tablespoons chopped onion
½ teaspoon horseradish
salt and pepper to taste
1 2-ounce package slivered almonds

Blend together cream cheese, milk, crab meat, onion, and horseradish. Add salt and pepper. Sprinkle almonds over top. Put in shallow baking dish and bake at 350 degrees for 20 minutes or until lightly browned on top. Serve hot, on crackers or as a dip.

These hors d'oeuvres may also be served without cooking if desired. If so, add milk to proper consistency for either a spread or a dip.

Maryland's Political Potluck Cookbook

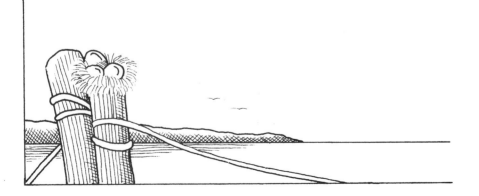

LINDA'S CRAB FINGERS SAUCE

½ cup mayonnaise

2 tablespoons spicy brown mustard

1 tablespoon horseradish

1 clove garlic, minced

1 tablespoon fresh parsley, chopped

1 teaspoon Old Bay Seasoning

4 dashes Tabasco sauce

Blend ingredients together thoroughly. Serve with crab fingers (cocktail crab claws) as a dip for an appetizer. Also great with shrimp cocktail or fried fish.

This dish always made a great impression during holiday dinners or parties, as a quick and easy way to start off a meal. Just spread crab fingers over crushed ice on a round platter with the sauce in the center for dipping.

Linda McBrearty, Beaverton, Oregon

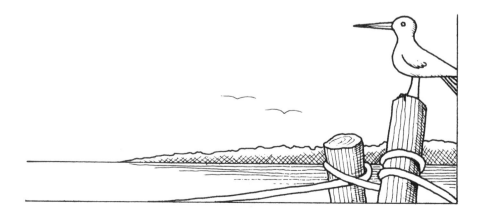

LONGFELLOWS PHYLLO TRIANGLES

2 pounds fresh spinach
3 pounds ricotta cheese
4 cloves fresh garlic
2 medium onions
2 pounds backfin crab meat
nutmeg to taste
salt and pepper to taste
phyllo pastry sheets
clarified butter

Destem, coarsely chop, and briefly steam the spinach. Drain and let cool. Chop and grind the garlic into a paste with salt to absorb some of the oils from the garlic. Chop the onions coarsely, saute lightly in clarified butter, and cool. Combine all ingredients except phyllo and let rest for 1 hour.

Lay out two sheets of phyllo and cut into five strips, making four cuts. Brush strips with clarified butter. Place 2 ounces of mixture in a ball at the bottom of each of the five strips. With each strip, fold from corner to corner until the end of the phyllo folds like a flag; continue folding, covering each edge of the triangle. Seal the ends with a brush of butter. Bake at 450 degrees for 8 to 10 minutes until lightly browned. Makes 60 2-ounce triangles.

This recipe is as great as an appetizer as it is as a main course. Either way, they all find a way to disappear.

Longfellows Restaurant, St. Michaels, Maryland

CRAB TARTS

pastry for 2-crust pie
3 large eggs, beaten
1½ cups skim milk
¾ cup Swiss cheese, grated
2 tablespoons cream cheese, softened
1 tablespoon onion, minced
¼ cup fresh parsley, chopped fine
½ cup carrots, shredded
1 pound regular crab meat
½ teaspoon nutmeg
¼ teaspoon white pepper
pinch salt

Roll out dough thinly and cut out 2-inch diameter circles with a cookie cutter. Lightly press dough circles into oiled tart shells. Prick dough with a fork. Bake for 5 to 7 minutes at 450 degrees. Remove from oven. Set aside. Mix together remaining ingredients and spoon into tart shells, filling them ½ inch over the top of the tart shell. Bake for 25 minutes at 375 degrees or until a toothpick inserted comes out clean. Serve hot. Yield: 60 tarts.

The delicate colors of carrots and parsley make these hors d'oeuvres attractive additions to any table.

Maryland Office of Seafood Marketing, Annapolis, Maryland

CRAB PATE WITH ALMONDS

¼ cup butter

½ cup chopped unblanched almonds

1 small onion, chopped

3 ounces cream cheese

8 ounces crab meat

1 tablespoon brandy

¼ teaspoon ground mace

Salt to taste

Melt the butter over medium heat in a small skillet. When it foams, add the almonds. Turn the heat to low and saute the almonds, stirring often, until they are golden brown. Remove them with a slotted spoon and reserve.

Cook the onion in the same butter, stirring often, until it is wilted and just starting to turn gold. Remove from pan. Reserve the butter.

Use a processor, blender, or mortar and pestle to crush the almonds and onions to a smooth paste.

In a small bowl, work the cream cheese until it is soft, then work in the almond and onion puree. Stir in the crab meat and seasonings, adding the reserved butter last.

Let the pate mellow for 15 minutes or so, then taste it and adjust the salt.

This pate will stay good for 3 or 4 days in the refrigerator. Let it come almost to room temperature before serving, then serve with crusty French bread.

Crab Collection

CRAB STUFFED CHERRY TOMATOES

30 ripe cherry tomatoes, washed
½ pound backfin crab meat
4 teaspoons plain, lowfat yogurt
3 teaspoons parsley, chopped
3 teaspoons onion, finely diced
1 teaspoon Worcestershire sauce
½ teaspoon seafood seasoning
⅛ teaspoon white pepper
pinch salt
parsley
paprika

Core tops of tomatoes, set aside. Combine remaining ingredients and mix gently. Spoon mixture into tomatoes, filling about ½ inch over tomato tops. Sprinkle lightly with paprika and parsley. Serve cold or hot. To heat, bake in a preheated 375-degree oven for 10 minutes. Yield: 30 tomatoes.

You, too, will capture a Maryland memory when you prepare this delightful down-home dish. We adapted this recipe from the Maryland Seafood Cookbook.

Maryland Department of Economic and Community Development

SPARROWS PT. BRANDIED CRAB

2 tablespoons butter
¼ cup fresh parsley, finely chopped
2 tablespoons brandy
⅛ teaspoon salt
⅛ teaspoon white pepper
pinch nutmeg
pinch paprika
1 large fresh lemon
1 pound backfin crab meat
crackers

In a large skillet or electric wok, melt butter. Add parsley, brandy, salt, white pepper, nutmeg, paprika, and the juice of one lemon. Heat until hot. Add crab meat and toss lightly to heat and coat. Be careful not to break up lumps. Serve in buffet dish with crackers on the side.

Brandy adds interest, flavor and excitement to the beginning foods you offer your guests.

Crab Collection

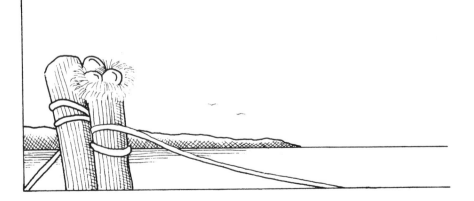

BAKED CRAB CASSEROLE

1 pound backfin crab meat
2 8-ounce packages cream cheese
½ pint sour cream
4 tablespoons mayonnaise
juice of ½ lemon
2 teaspoons Worcestershire sauce
1 teaspoon dry mustard
¼ teaspoon garlic salt
½ cup grated cheddar cheese

Soften cheese to room temperature. Mix ingredients in the order listed. Add only ¼ cup of the grated cheese to mixture. Sprinkle the remaining ¼ cup on top. Bake at 350 degrees for 45 to 50 minutes. Serve with crackers.

Eastern shore hospitality reigns supreme in Salisbury, Maryland, and it was at the Salisbury In-Water Boat Show that this recipe was prepared.

Spengler and Barbara Womack, Salisbury, Maryland

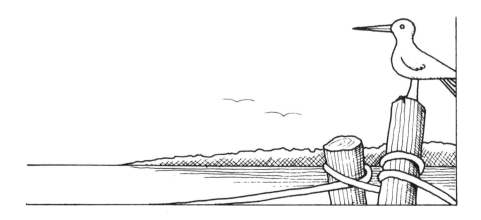

HOT CRAB DIP IN BREAD BASKET

2 8-ounce packages cream cheese, softened

½ cup mayonnaise

¼ cup dry white wine

2 green onions, chopped

2 cloves garlic, minced

½ teaspoon Worcestershire sauce

1 pound crab meat

¼ cup chopped pimiento

2-pound round loaf of bread, wheat or rye

In small bowl, mix and beat cream cheese until fluffy. Gradually beat in mayonnaise, wine, green onions, garlic, and Worcestershire sauce until smooth and well blended. Stir in crab and pimiento. Slice off top of bread loaf. Scoop out center of loaf to make basket. Place bread on baking sheet; fill center with crab mixture. Bake about 45 minutes at 350 degrees, until very warm. Serve with crackers or fresh vegetables.

This recipe was clipped from the local paper and was an overwhelming success when served at a recent dinner party. Give it a try. I'm sure you will agree.

Capital Newspaper, Annapolis, Maryland

CRAB BACON CANAPE

¼ cup tomato juice
1 well-beaten egg
½ pound crab meat
½ cup fine dry bread crumbs
1 tablespoon parsley
1 tablespoon lemon juice
¼ teaspoon Worcestershire sauce
¼ teaspoon salt
9 slices bacon, cut in half

Mix tomato juice and egg. Add crab meat, bread crumbs, parsley, lemon juice, salt, and Worcestershire sauce. Mix well. Roll into 18 fingers, 2 inches long. Wrap each with ½ slice bacon; secure with toothpick. Broil 5 inches from heat for 10 minutes, turning to brown. Serves 18.

These handsome fingersize sandwiches are hearty with robust flavor. Garnish with red tomato or pimiento and serve with your favorite beverage.

Scott and Johanna Brudvig, Richmond, Virginia

QUICKIE CRAB PICKERS SPREAD

1 pound crab meat
1 package (6 to 10 ounces) Italian salad
   dressing mix
1 cup sour cream
½ cup mayonnaise or salad dressing
1 tablespoon horseradish mustard
chopped parsley (garnish)
assorted chips, crackers, or raw vegetables

Remove any shell or cartilage from crab meat. Combine crab meat, salad dressing mix, sour cream, mayonnaise, and horseradish mustard; chill if desired. Garnish with parsley. Serve with crackers, chips, or vegetables. Makes approximately 3 cups spread.

Try this recipe for the hostess who needs easy-to-prepare and delicious seafood ideas.

Florida Department of Natural Resources, Bureau of Marketing and Extension Services

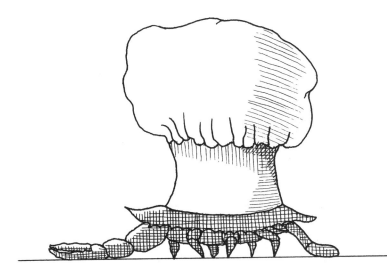

NEW ORLEANS CRAB SPREAD

1 pound crab meat

¼ cup tarragon vinegar

⅓ cup mayonnaise

3 tablespoons chopped pimiento

2 tablespoons chopped green onion

1 teaspoon salt

½ teaspoon freshly ground pepper

1 tablespoon drained capers

assorted chips, crackers, or raw vegetables

Remove shell or cartilage from crab meat. Flake the crab meat. Pour vinegar over crab meat. Chill for 30 minutes. Drain. Add mayonnaise, pimiento, onion, salt, and pepper. Mix thoroughly. Garnish with capers. Serve with chips, crackers, or vegetables. Makes approximately 2 cups.

The use of homemade tarragon vinegar adds a special touch to this spread. Decorate with fresh tarragon leaves and serve well chilled. It's mighty good.

Crab Collection

ANNIE'S CRAB MEAT SPREAD

1 cup crab meat, flaked
½ tablespoon lemon juice
8 ounces cream cheese, softened
⅛ teaspoon salt
dash pepper
½ teaspoon dry mustard
3 tablespoons mayonnaise
dash Tabasco
paprika

Place all ingredients in blender and mix well. Arrange in small serving bowl, sprinkle with paprika. Chill and serve with crackers, party rye bread, or small bread sticks.

This appetizer is easy to make up ahead of time. Serve it as a snack with beverages. It is luscious.

Annie Hendricks, Alexandria, Virginia

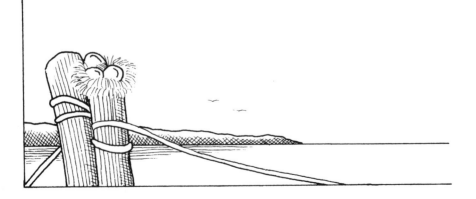

HAMMOND'S CRAB DIP

3 packages (8 ounces each) cream cheese
¼ to ½ cup milk
1 pound crab meat
¼ cup chopped green onions with tops
1 teaspoon horseradish
2 teaspoons Worcestershire sauce

Combine all in lightly greased crock pot. Cover and cook on high until mixture is smooth. Add more milk if needed.

Good food and good friends are always a winning combination. Try this recipe and your friends will be delighted.

Carol Hammond, Bowie, Maryland

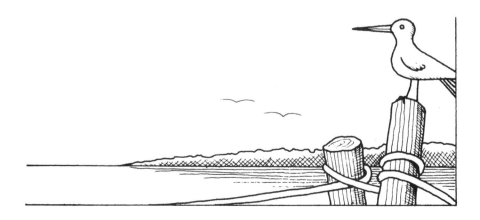

ELAINE'S CRAB DIP

7½ 8-ounce packages cream cheese mashed
with ½ cup mayonnaise
add dash garlic powder
2 teaspoons prepared mustard
dash Lowry salt
2 teaspoons confectionery sugar
fold in 2½ pounds crab meat
add ⅔ cup white Rhine wine

Mix ingredients and heat in double boiler until smooth. Serve in chafing dish. Serves a crowd.

There's always need for a crab dip that will serve a large group. This classic addition will calm any crowd.

Elaine Cohen, Olney, Maryland

LEE'S HOT CRAB DIP

1 8-ounce package cream cheese, softened
½ cup sour cream
2 tablespoons mayonnaise
1 tablespoon lemon juice
1¼ teaspoon Worcestershire sauce
½ teaspoon dry mustard
pinch garlic salt
1 tablespoon milk
¼ cup cheddar cheese, grated
½ pound regular crab meat
paprika for garnish

Remove cartilage from crab meat. In a large bowl, mix cream cheese, sour cream, mayonnaise, lemon juice, Worcestershire sauce, mustard, and garlic salt until smooth. Add enough milk to make mixture creamy. Stir in 2 tablespoons of the grated cheese. Fold crab meat into cream cheese mixture. Pour into greased 1-quart casserole. Top with remaining cheese and paprika. Bake at 325 degrees until mixture is bubbly and browned on top, about 30 minutes. Yield: about 4 cups dip.

Dry mustard and cheddar cheese give a sharp flavor to this baked dip. Serve with crackers or French bread chunks.

Lee Schmidt, Upper Marlboro, Maryland

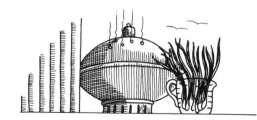

DEBBIE'S DIP

½ pound crab meat
1 8-ounce package cream cheese
½ cup sour cream
2 tablespoons mayonnaise
1 tablespoon lemon juice
1¼ teaspoon Worcestershire sauce
½ teaspoon dry mustard
½ teaspoon garlic salt
1 tablespoon milk
1 teaspoon McCormick seafood seasoning

Combine all ingredients; mix well. Bake at 350 degrees for about ½ hour. Serve hot over pastries or chill and use as a dip.

Hot or cold this dip is surely a crab lover's delight.

Debbie Bolton, Dunkirk, Maryland

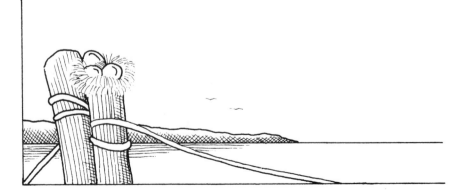

JONES POINT CREAMY CRAB DIP

½ pound crab meat
8-ounce package cream cheese
3 tablespoons white wine
1 teaspoon horseradish sauce
3 tablespoons minced onion
1 teaspoon Worcestershire sauce
paprika

Soften cream cheese and mix with remaining ingredients. Place in pie plate or shallow casserole. Sprinkle with paprika and bake about 15 minutes at 350 degrees, until bubbly. Serve with crackers or toast.

This recipe can be made ahead of time and refrigerated until ready to reheat and serve.

Crab Collection

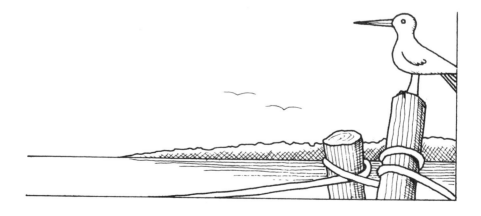

SWING'S CRAB DIP

1 pound cooked shrimp, cooled and shelled
1 pound crab meat
1 cup butter
1 cup chopped green onions
1 small can mushrooms
1 cup all-purpose flour
1 6-ounce can evaporated milk
2 cups milk
1 cup fresh parsley
1 teaspoon paprika
½ teaspoon pepper
salt to taste

Cut shrimp in small pieces and combine with crab meat. Melt butter in a 2-quart saucepan. Saute onions until soft and saute mushrooms briefly. Stir in flour until smooth and cook until thickened slightly. Slowly stir in evaporated milk and milk, stirring constantly. Cook until smooth and thickened. Add shrimp and crab and seasonings. Serve hot with corn chips. Makes about 1 quart dip.

This recipe is quick and easy to prepare and it's one that always brings raves.

Bud Swing, The Catered Crab, Annapolis, Maryland

PRINCESS ANNE CRAB DIP

¼ pound butter
2 8-ounce blocks of cream cheese
1 pound crab meat
Tabasco and Worcestershire sauce to taste

Melt butter in a chafing or fondue dish. Add cheese and let melt, stirring occasionally. Fold in crab meat, add Tabasco and Worcestershire sauce to taste. Serve hot on crackers or melba toast directly from dish. Continue to stir occasionally. Serves 16 to 20.

You may want to enjoy this dish with your favorite potato chip. I bet you can't eat just one.

Crab Collection

DOWN NECKER DIP

¾ cup mayonnaise
½ cup sour cream
2 tablespoons finely chopped parsley
½ pound crab meat
1 tablespoon sherry
1 teaspoon lemon juice
dash salt

Combine mayonnaise, sour cream, chopped parsley, crab meat, sherry, lemon juice, and salt. Chill several hours or overnight. Serve with raw vegetables or chips.

Probably the most important step is to let the flavors blend. Using fresh, crisp vegetables is also an important step. The results are incredibly delicious.

Crisfield Bill and Gracie, Crisfield, Maryland

CRUNCHY CRAB NUGGETS

1 1-pound loaf Vienna or French bread
1 stick butter, melted
½ pound Maryland crab meat
⅔ cup American process cheese spread
1 large egg
1 teaspoon Worcestershire sauce
¼ teaspoon lemon and pepper seasoning
⅛ teaspoon dry mustard
2 to 3 dashes garlic powder
paprika for garnish

Cut bread into 1-inch slices; remove crusts. Cut trimmed slices into 1 ½-inch cubes. Hollow out each cube with sharp knife, leaving a shell about ⅛-inch thick. Brush sides and tops with melted butter. Place on cookie sheet(s).

Bake at 400 degrees for 10 minutes or until nuggets are lightly browned and crisp. Remove from oven and cool.

In a bowl, blend cheese and egg. Add Worcestershire sauce, lemon and pepper seasoning, mustard, and garlic powder; gently mix in crab meat.

Fill nuggets with crab meat mixture; sprinkle paprika over tops. Put on cookie sheet(s) and bake at 400 degrees until hot and bubbly, 5 to 10 minutes. Makes 4 dozen crab nuggets.

If desired, cocktail canape shells may be substituted for nuggets. Crab meat mixture will make 3 dozen canapes.

Seafood Marketing Authority, Annapolis, Maryland

Crab Soups

HAWK COVE CRAB SOUP

2 cups milk

¼ teaspoon ground mace

¼ teaspoon dry mustard

⅛ teaspoon ground nutmeg

2 teaspoons grated lemon peel

1 pound crab meat

2 cups half and half

3 tablespoons butter

½ teaspoon salt

½ cup dry white wine

¼ cup cracker crumbs

Combine milk, spices, and lemon peel in top of a large double boiler; stir well. Cook mixture over simmering water 10 minutes.

Stir crab meat, half and half, butter, and salt into hot mixture; cook over boiling water 20 minutes, stirring often. Stir in wine and cracker crumbs. Serve immediately. Yield: 4 to 6 servings.

Here's an easy-to-prepare, attractive, and delicious soup that's certain to please guests of all ages.

Crab Collection

TRED AVON CREAM OF CRAB SOUP

1 pound lump crab meat
1 pint of milk
1 pint of cream
½ stick of butter
½ teaspoon ground mace
2 pieces of lemon peel
¼ cup of cracker crumbs
salt and pepper to taste
2 tablespoons of sherry

Put milk in top of double boiler with mace and lemon peel and allow to simmer for a few minutes. Remove the lemon peel. Then add crab, butter, and cream and cook for 15 minutes. Thicken with cracker crumbs. Season with salt and pepper. Just before serving, add sherry. Serves 6.

This recipe is rich, and the refreshing, mild flavor of the lemon and mace makes it an ideal summer dish.

The Official Crab Eater's Guide

EASTERN SHORE CREAM OF CRAB

3 cups milk

¼ pound butter

1 pound lump crab meat

3 tablespoons celery, chopped

1 tablespoon parsley

1 teaspoon salt

⅛ teaspoon pepper

2 teaspoons flour

¼ cup water

½ cup light cream

Scald milk, add butter, and heat until melted. Add crab, celery, parsley, salt and pepper. Simmer 15 minutes. Blend flour and water and add to mixture. Cook until thick. Add cream and mix well. Simmer 20 minutes. Serves 6.

This luscious concoction attests to the innovativeness of eastern shore chefs. Do not let the dish wait for your diners; it should be eaten immediately.

Lois Lane, Glen Burnie, Maryland

CREAM OF CRAB AND ASPARAGUS SOUP

1 stick butter

2 tablespoons chopped onion

¼ cup all-purpose flour

4 cups milk

2 tablespoons chopped onion

2 teaspoons parsley flakes

½ teaspoon salt

¼ teaspoon nutmeg

1 pound crab meat (backfin preferred)

2 teaspoons chicken bouillon powder

½ teaspoon pepper (white pepper preferred)

½ to 1 teaspoon Old Bay Seafood Seasoning

½ pound asparagus (fresh or frozen—drain and thaw well)

In saucepan, melt butter over medium to low heat. Add onions and saute until onions are tender. Whisk in flour slowly. After this has been mixed well, whisk milk in slowly. Add all remaining ingredients (except crab meat and asparagus) and cook until mixture thickens. If this mixture becomes too thick, add a little milk. When desired consistency is reached, add crab meat and asparagus. Cook only until asparagus is crisp and tender (about 10 to 15 minutes). Serve immediately. Season to taste. Makes about 8 cups.

This recipe was the first prize winner in the 1988 Holiday Cookbook Recipe Contest, The Daily Banner, Cambridge, Maryland. We congratulate the winner. You will, too.

Steve Willey, Cambridge, Maryland

ANNIE'S CREAM OF CRAB SOUP

½ cup of butter
½ cup of flour
2 tablespoons chicken bouillon crystals
dash of white pepper
1 quart of milk
salt
½ pound backfin crab meat

Check over crab meat for bits of shell and cartilage. Melt butter, blend in flour and pepper. Stir—simmer for 2 minutes. Add milk and chicken crystals. Simmer and stir until bouillon is absorbed and mixture thickens enough to coat spoon.

Salt to taste, add crab meat, heat but do not boil. Serves 4 to 5.

To serve later, refrigerate, then reheat over low heat. Stir often, but do not boil.

Annie Hendricks, Alexandria, Virginia

CHILLED CREAM OF CRAB SOUP

1 container frozen avocado dip
½ pound crab meat
¼ cup minced red bell pepper
½ cup minced celery
1 cup sour cream
1 cup heavy cream
Tabasco, salt, and white pepper to taste
toasted almonds

Combine all ingredients and chill thoroughly. If too thick, thin with more heavy cream. Serve in saucer-type champagne or parfait glasses. Makes 6 servings.

Vicki H. D'Andrea of Millersville, Maryland received honorable mention in The Sunday Capital's 1988 soup contest for this recipe. Congratulations! Vicki, we loved it.

Capital Newspaper, Annapolis, Maryland

QUICK CREAMED CRAB SOUP

2 tablespoons butter

3 tablespoons finely chopped green pepper

4 tablespoons chopped onion

1 (10½ ounce) can cream of mushroom soup

¼ cup sherry

½ pound crab meat

buttered toast or cooked rice or crisp chow mein noodles

parsley

Melt butter in saucepan. Add green pepper and onion; saute 3 minutes. Stir in undiluted soup and sherry; mix well. Add crab. Heat until steaming, stirring gently to avoid breaking crab pieces. Serve over hot toast, rice or noodles. Sprinkle with parsley. Makes 2 cups, serves 2 to 4.

This delightful soup is also superb over an omelet. For a special occasion, try substituting lobster in place of crab.

Crab Collection

ELEGANT CRAB SOUP

2 tablespoons butter
1½ tablespoons flour
2½ cups milk
1 teaspoon salt
¼ teaspoon black pepper
¼ teaspoon red pepper
1 pound crab meat
1 cup cream
1 hard-boiled egg
sherry to taste (about a wine glass)

Melt butter in a saucepan and stir in flour, then the milk, salt, and peppers. Stir until well-heated and thickened. Add the crab meat and cream. Heat well. Add the egg, pressing it through a sieve. Add sherry and correct seasonings, adding more salt and red pepper if necessary. Serves 6.

This dish should never be underestimated. It is simple, tasteful, and delightful.

Country Magazine, February 1981

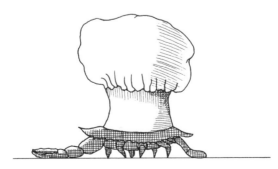

HARBOUR HOUSE CREAM OF CRAB SOUP

1 pound Maryland backfin crab meat
4 tablespoons butter
⅓ cup flour
1 cup chicken broth
¼ teaspoon pepper
5 cups milk
salt to taste

Pick over crab meat carefully to remove any shell or cartilage. Melt butter in a 3-quart pan. Blend in flour and stir until smooth. Slowly stir in chicken broth and pepper and simmer for 2 minutes, until slightly thickened. Add milk and cook slowly, stirring constantly, until thickened. Do not boil. Add crab meat to milk mixture and salt to taste. Remove from heat and serve. Makes about 10 cups.

Maryland crab is the pride of the Chesapeake; so it's no surprise that the State promotes seafood. This recipe is featured in the Maryland Seafood Cookbook No. 2, put out by the Seafood Marketing Authority. But visit The Harbour House yourself and give this classic version a try.

Harbour House Restaurant, Annapolis, Maryland

CRAB POT INN CRAB BISQUE

2 tablespoons butter
½ cup diced onion
½ cup diced celery
1 pound fresh lump crab meat
1 tablespoon Old Bay Seafood Seasoning
¼ pound chedder cheese, shredded
¼ pound diced fresh shrimp
¼ pound fresh chopped mushrooms
1 teaspoon parsley
1½ cups milk
½ cup sherry

Melt butter and saute ½ cup diced onion and ½ cup diced celery in skillet and add the remaining ingredients. Simmer until steaming. Serves 6 to 8.

This thick, rich soup, whether served alone or as part of a complete meal, is sure to be a conversation piece. I have found it to be perfectly reheatable for a late night snack.

Richard and Bernice Harrison, Crab Pot Inn, Chipley, Florida

SOLOMONS CRAB STEW

1 dozen steamed blue crabs
½ cup finely chopped celery
1 tablespoon finely chopped onion or chives
3 tablespoons butter
1 (10¾ ounce) can cream of mushroom
    soup, undiluted
1 cup milk
salt and pepper to taste
1 to 2 teaspoons cooking sherry
lemon slices

Remove meat from bodies and claws of crabs. Saute celery and onion in butter; add crab meat, mushroom soup, and milk. Cook over low heat for 15 to 20 minutes, stirring frequently. Season to taste with salt and pepper.

Before serving, add sherry. Garnish with lemon slices. Yield: 4 servings.

This recipe is an impressive yet simple favorite with our guests. It will equal any crab stew served in a restaurant. Everyone who tastes it loves it.

Crab Collection

CRAB STEW

1 cup olive oil

1½ cups all-purpose flour

½ pound sweet green pepper, chopped

1 large pod garlic, minced

1 pod red pepper, crushed

3 large onions, chopped

3 stalks celery, chopped

1 dozen large crabs

salt to taste

chopped parsley

chopped green onion tops

hot cooked rice

Put olive oil in large iron pot; heat thoroughly, and stir in flour. Cook over very low heat for about 30 minutes, stirring constantly so flour does not brown. Add green pepper, garlic, red pepper, onion, and celery; cook slowly for about 20 minutes, stirring once or twice. Add crabs, which have been cleaned and cut into halves (reserve the crab fat and claw meat). Stir well; add salt to taste and cover pot.

Do not add water at any time; cook slowly for 30 minutes; then add crab fat and meat from crab claws. Simmer 15 minutes longer with pot covered. When ready to serve, sprinkle freely with chopped parsley and green onion tops. Serve with hot cooked rice. Yield: 8 servings.

This is a hearty dish, especially soothing during the cold winter months. Accompany it with home made hush puppies and a green salad.

Crab Collection

BOHEMIA RIVER CRAB STEW

1 leek

1 onion

8 ribs celery

¼ pound butter

2 tablespoons flour

1 teaspoon tomato paste

pinch of oregano

1 quart chicken broth

1 quart fish stock

4 ounces crab roe

½ pound crab meat

4 tablespoons sherry

1 teaspoon Worcestershire sauce

salt and pepper to taste

2 egg yolks, beaten

½ pint cream

Dice vegetables. Melt butter in saucepan; add vegetables and simmer until tender. Add flour, tomato paste and oregano; stir well. Stir in chicken broth and fish stock, then boil for 30 minutes, stirring occasionally. Add crab roe, crab meat, sherry, Worcestershire sauce, salt, and pepper. Cook for 5 minutes, then remove from heat. Add egg yolks and cream. Serve at once. Makes about 1 gallon.

From the top of the Bay to Pirate's Cove, Charleston, South Carolina, this special soup will earn a spot in every kitchen.

Crab Collection

G.W.'S SHE CRAB SOUP

1 pound crab meat with crab eggs
2 tablespoons butter
2 medium yellow onions, minced
1 tablespoon flour
1 quart hot milk
salt and pepper to taste
pinch nutmeg
4 ounces dry sherry
8 ounces heavy cream

Melt the butter in a large skillet and saute the onions until they are soft. Add the crab meat and crab eggs. Saute for a few seconds. Sprinkle the flour over the crab mixture and stir until the flour blends with the butter. Add the hot milk gradually, stirring constantly.

Simmer very slowly for 20 minutes. Season with salt, pepper and nutmeg. Add the sherry and cream. Heat to just below the boiling point. Serves 6.

George Washington was served rich, creamy she crab soup during a visit to Charleston, South Carolina in 1791. What makes this soup so special is the addition of the richly flavored roe or eggs of the female crab.

The Official Crab Eater's Guide

SOUTHERN CRAB GUMBO SUPREME

1 whole chicken, cut up
1 pound shrimp
1 quart oysters
2 tablespoons okra
1 onion
1 clove garlic
1 pound sliced ham
1 pound crab meat
1 can tomatoes
1 bay leaf
1 green pepper
salt and pepper

Boil chicken with bay leaf, salt and pepper and onion until tender. Remove, cut in large pieces and return to stock. Cut and fry ham in small pieces with green pepper and garlic and add to stock. Add can of tomatoes, okra, cut up fine, and raw shrimp. When okra is tender, add crab meat and oysters. Let boil 5 minutes or until oysters are plump. Serve in soup plates on fluffy white cooked rice. Serves 12.

Try a light red wine, such as a Beaujolais or California Gamay, to complement this robust gumbo.

Crab Collection

HEARTY CRAB SOUP

4 cups cold water
1 cup diced carrots
1 cup chopped onion
¾ cup chopped celery
¼ cup butter
1 tablespoon seafood seasoning
1 tablespoon Worcestershire sauce
1½ cups diced potatoes
1 1-pound can tomatoes, chopped
2 tablespoons parsley
1 tablespoon flour (mixed with ⅓ cup water to thicken)
1 pound Maryland special crab meat

Put water in large pot and bring to boil. Add all ingredients except crab meat and flour mixture. Bring to boil then simmer 1½ hours. Thicken with flour mixture. Add crab meat, simmer ½ hour. Yields 1½ quarts.

This recipe can easily be doubled for serving a group. Serve with a soda bread or dark pumpernickel and listen to the comments. Wonderful!

Recipe developed by the Seafood Marketing Authority, Annapolis, Maryland

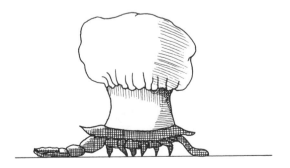

BAY COUNTRY CRAB SOUP

1 pound beef shin, bone-in

3 quarts water

1 large onion, chopped

2 large stalks celery, chopped

1 1-pound can tomatoes

1 tablespoon salt

¼ teaspoon black pepper

⅛ teaspoon cayenne pepper

1 10-ounce package frozen mixed vegetables

1 pound Maryland regular crab meat

½ pound Maryland claw crab meat

Place the first eight ingredients in a large pan and simmer, covered, until meat is very tender, about 3 hours. Add the rest of the ingredients and simmer, covered, until vegetables are done. Makes about 5 quarts soup.

Few recipes establish a cook's reputation as well as a recipe for a flavorful crab soup. Try this bountiful Bay rendition. It's truly a name maker.

Recipe developed by the Seafood Marketing Authority, Annapolis, Maryland

SPICY CRAB SOUP

1 quart water

3 chicken parts (necks or wings)

3 pounds canned tomatoes, quartered

8 ounces fresh or frozen corn, drained

1 cup fresh or frozen peas, drained

1 cup potatoes, pared and diced

¾ cup celery, chopped

¾ cup onion, diced

¾ tablespoon Old Bay Seasoning

1 teaspoon salt

¼ teaspoon lemon pepper

1 pound Maryland crab meat

Place water and chicken in a 6-quart soup pot. Cover and simmer over low heat for at least one hour. Add vegetables and seasonings; cover and simmer over medium low heat for about 45 minutes or until vegetables are almost done. Add crab meat, cover and simmer for 15 more minutes or until hot. Remove chicken skin and larger bones. Serves 6 to 8.

Marylanders would never do it, but if a milder soup is desired, decrease Old Bay Seasoning.

The Washington Times Magazine, June 20, 1983

CLAW-OYSTER STEW

1 pound claw meat
1 pint fresh shucked oysters and liquor
¾ stick butter
2 tablespoons fresh lemon thyme
1 quart half and half

Melt butter in large cooking pot. Add crab meat. Add oysters. Cook thoroughly until the oysters curl. Add half and half and lemon thyme. Cook until stew is hot, but don't boil. Serve with corn bread. Serves 6 to 8.

More and more people are discovering the delicate taste of oyster and crab. If you've never before tasted this fabulous combination, claw-oyster stew is a great way to start. It's a rich and satisfying dish for an informal brunch or supper.

Crab Collection

MARYLAND CRAB SOUP SUPREME

1 large soup bone
12 crab bodies and claws, cleaned
3 quarts water
2 large stalks celery, chopped
1 large can tomatoes
¼ small head cabbage, chopped
1 green pepper, chopped
⅛ teaspoon cayenne pepper
salt and pepper to taste
1 pound crab meat
1 pound claw crab meat
1 large frozen mixed vegetables
sherry

Put first ten ingredients in large pot and simmer for about an hour. Add crab meat and frozen vegetables and simmer until vegetables are tender. Add sherry just before serving. Serves 10.

A flavorful medley of crabs and vegetables combine to make this hearty soup a classic. Serve with a red wine and you will learn how seafood and grapes can complement each other.

Crab Collection

CRAB BISQUE CHINCOTEAGUE

4 tablespoons butter
4 tablespoons flour
4 cups milk
¾ cup sharp cheddar cheese
2 teaspoons seafood seasoning
½ teaspoon lemon pepper
2 tablespoons cooking sherry
1 pint whipping cream
1 tablespoon chopped parsley
    salt to taste
1 pound lump crab meat

Melt butter in a heavy 4-quart saucepan over medium heat. Stir in flour to make a roux. Slowly add milk until it is well blended. Stirring constantly, add cheese and cook until mixture thickens. Reduce heat and add seasonings, sherry, cream, and parsley. When mixture is thoroughly heated, add crab meat, stirring gently to keep lumps intact. Serve immediately in warm bowls and garnish with parsley. Serves 6.

The cook's preference here is a very dry, firm white wine such as a California Gewurztraminer or Sauvignon Blanc for this recipe.

Crab Collection

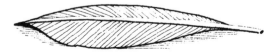

BALTIMORE CRAB SOUP

To 1 gallon of very hot water, add:

> 1 pound stew beef, diced and browned with fat
>
> 4 beef bouillon cubes
>
> 1 teaspoon salt
>
> ¼ teaspoon pepper
>
> 1 tablespoon seafood seasoning
>
> 3 slices bacon, halved
>
> 1 whole stalk celery, diced
>
> 1 large can tomato paste or catsup

Cook 1 hour over high heat in an uncovered pot.

> Add:
>
> 2 packages mixed frozen vegetables
>
> 3 large potatoes, diced
>
> 1 large onion, diced
>
> 1 small cabbage, shredded
>
> ¼ cup barley

Cook for 1 hour over medium heat.

> Add:
>
> 1 pound regular crab meat
>
> 1 pound claw crab meat

The origin of this recipe is unknown, but we have used it many times and it's mighty good.

Crab Collection

DUNGENESS CRAB VICHYSSOISE

2 bunches, leeks, cleaned and chopped

2 pounds potatoes, sliced

1 gallon fish stock

6 ounces Dungeness Crab meat

1 quart heavy cream

6 Dungeness crab legs

salt

white pepper

Worcestershire sauce

Tabasco sauce

chives or green onions, chopped

Combine first three ingredients plus Dungeness crab meat in soup pot. Simmer until potatoes are quite done. Run through food processor with steel blade until pureed. Chill. When chilled, stir in heavy cream and add salt, white pepper, Worcestershire sauce and Tabasco to taste. Place 1 Dungeness crab leg in each serving bowl, fill with soup and top with chives. Must be served very cold. Serves 6.

This recipe was sent to me by the Oregon Dungeness Crab Commission. It was featured in a collection of recipes entitled "Get Cracking with Dungeness Crab." We give credit to the chef.

Carl Karaust, Silver Garden Restaurant, Portland, Oregon

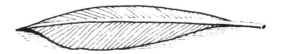

CORRINE'S SPICY CRAB SOUP

3 quarts water

1 large can V-8 juice

1 pound can crushed tomatoes

1 pound mixed crab meat

1 large onion, diced

½ cup celery, diced

1 tablespoon salt

½ teaspoon black pepper

2 tablespoons Old Bay Seasoning (more to suit taste)

⅛ teaspoon cayenne pepper

1 tablespoon oregano

4 cups mixed fresh vegetables (potatoes, carrots, corn, string beans) cut into bite-size pieces. You can substitute fresh vegetables for the following: 1 medium can of each—kernel corn, cut green beans, carrots, potatoes, which you will add to cooked soup the last 10 minutes of cooking.

Fill a large pot with water, juice, tomatoes, seasonings, and fresh vegetables. Simmer until veggies are tender. Add crab meat and simmer an additional 15 minutes before serving. Serves 8 to 10.

Corrine's recipe is a must to try if you are sailing the Bay or camping in L.A.

"The Galley Kiss Cookbook," Corrine C. Kanter

CORN AND CRAB CHOWDER

3 slices bacon

½ onion, finely chopped

½ cup chopped celery

½ green pepper, finely chopped

½ red pepper, finely chopped

½ cup raw, peeled, finely diced potatoes

2 cups water

¼ teaspoon paprika

bay leaf

3 tablespoons flour

2 cups milk

2 cups cooked corn

½ pound crab meat

Saute the bacon until very crisp. Remove and crumble. In the bacon drippings, saute onion, celery and peppers until onion is soft, but not brown. Add the water, bay leaf, paprika, and potatoes and simmer until the potatoes are tender (35-40 minutes).

Bring just to the boiling point and add the flour and ½ cup of the milk.

In a separate saucepan, heat crab meat, corn, and the remaining milk. When warmed through (but not boiling), add this and the bacon to the soup mixture. Heat gently for a few minutes, being careful not to boil. Garnish with fresh parsley, if desired. Serves 6.

This soup was featured in Chesapeake Bay Magazine's Galley Time, March 1986.

Cheryl Mandala

MARYLAND CRAB-CORN STEW

1 medium onion, chopped

2 cups potatoes, peeled and diced

2 cups water

½ teaspoon dried oregano

½ teaspoon salt

⅛ teaspoon white pepper

1 pound regular crab meat

1 cup whole-kernel corn

1 large tomato, peeled and chopped

1 medium green pepper, cleaned and chopped

few drops hot sauce

1½ cups half and half

⅓ cup chopped fresh parsley

Put onion, potatoes, water, oregano, salt, and white pepper in a large saucepan. Bring to a boil. Lower heat and cook slowly, covered, 25 minutes or until potatoes are tender. Mix in crab meat, corn, tomato, green pepper, and hot sauce. Continue cooking 5 minutes. Add half and half and parsley. Leave over low heat long enough to heat through. Serves 6.

This colorful stew with corn, tomato, and green pepper makes a lovely luncheon entree or a first course dinner. Prepare a green salad to accompany this dish and turn your meal into something special.

Crab Collection

LIZ'S CRAB SOUP

16 ounces chicken broth

1 quart half-and-half

1 stick butter

⅓ cup flour

2 medium shallots, chopped fine

1 teaspoon lemon pepper

½ teaspoon Old Bay Seasoning

½ cup white wine

1 pound backfin crab meat

2 tablespoons fresh parsley, chopped fine

¼ cup sherry

Saute shallots in butter until soft. Slowly add flour to make roux. Meanwhile, heat chicken broth, half-and-half, lemon pepper, Old Bay, and white wine. When heated thoroughly, combine a small amount of broth mixture to roux. Stir until smooth and pourable. Then add to broth and simmer gently until thickened. Just before serving, add crab meat, parsley, and sherry. Stir gently until combined and heated through. Serves 8.

Wasn't it yesterday, we drove to Popes Creek...and picked crabs, oh so sweet?

Liz Parness, Seabrook, Maryland

Crab Salads

BLUE CRAB REMOULADE

1 pound fresh backfin crab meat
¼ cup tarragon-flavored wine vinegar
2 tablespoons hot mustard
2 teaspoons prepared horseradish
1½ teaspoons paprika
2 tablespoons olive oil
⅓ cup minced green onions
⅓ cup shredded garden zucchini
2 tablespoons minced parsley
¼ teaspoon salt
⅛ teaspoon pepper

Combine the vinegar, mustard, horseradish, and spices in a small mixing bowl. Dribble the oil into the mixture while beating it all together with an electric mixer, so that the oil emulsifies with the mustard and vinegar. Stir in the minced and shredded vegetables.

Carefully pick through the crab meat to remove any overlooked cartilage. Gently incorporate the crab meat into the mixture, being careful not to break up the lumps of crab. Serves 6.

Blue Crab Remoulade is a simple dish that seems elegant and can be served in a variety of settings. Try it stuffed in a hollowed-out Maryland tomato, bell pepper, or a split avocado.

Jeffrey Holland, Bay Sailor Magazine

CAPTAIN SPARK'S CRAB SALAD

1 pound regular crab meat
¼ cup chopped celery
8 stuffed ripe olives, chopped
½ cup mayonnaise
1 teaspoon prepared mustard
small amount chopped onion
salt and pepper to taste
lettuce

Mix well and serve on lettuce leaf. Serves 4.

Stuffed and chopped, olives add a colorful twist to this simple salad. It's good any time of year.

Dorchester Crab Company, Wingate, Maryland

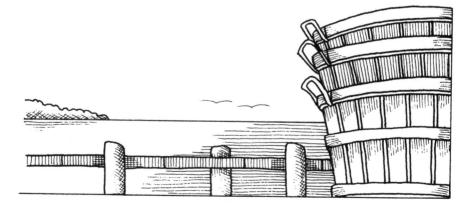

RAYMOND'S CRAB SALAD

1 pound crab meat

¾ cup chopped celery (2 to 3 stalks)

2 tablespoons lemon juice

1 teaspoon salt

⅛ teaspoon pepper

3 tablespoons mayonnaise

1 teaspoon capers

Remove all cartilage from crab meat. Put celery in bowl. Mix in lemon juice, salt, pepper, mayonnaise and capers. Add crab meat and mix gently but thoroughly. Serves 4.

An old lady who was celebrating her 100th birthday was being interviewed by a reporter who asked if there was any one thing to which she attributed her wonderful age. The old lady thought for a moment and then answered, "Yes, I think there is—crab salad."

Crab Collection

SHERRY'S SALAD

1 pound crab meat
⅓ stalk celery
mayonnaise to taste
1 tablespoon Old Bay Seasoning
¼ cup lemon juice

Mix ingredients together. Chill, and put in center of quartered home-grown tomatoes. Serves 4.

With our increased awareness of the importance of vegetables in our daily menus, salads of all types have become firmly established in our basic diet. The year-round availability and variety of fresh, crisp greens and tomatoes has made the salad bowl easy to prepare. Sherry's use of home-grown tomatoes in this recipe is a must.

Sherry Bresnahan, Skipper's Pier, Deale, Maryland

FALISHA'S CRAB SALAD

½ pound picked-over crab meat
1 tablespoon minced capers
3 water chestnuts, sliced
2 hard-cooked eggs (whites only), sliced thin
4 pickled cocktail onions, diced
2 tablespoons minced celery

FALISHA'S DRESSING

1 cup mayonnaise
1 teaspoon pepper
1 teaspoon caper juice
3 teaspoons beet juice
1 teaspoon cocktail onion juice
1 teaspoon cayenne pepper

Mix together ingredients for dressing and set aside. Mix together ingredients for salad, cover with dressing, toss, and refrigerate at least 2 hours. Serves 4.

A skillful mix of colors, shapes, textures, and flavors can make a salad tray properly festive and party perfect.

Alice Treutler, Chipley, Florida

EXOTIC CRAB MEAT SALAD

¼ cup chili sauce
⅔ cup mayonnaise
½ cup lemon juice, divided
½ teaspoon salt
1 pound crab meat
1 cup chopped celery
1 cup chopped Brazil nuts
lettuce
2 ripe avocados, sliced

Combine chili sauce, mayonnaise, 2 tablespoons lemon juice, and salt in a small bowl. Add crab meat, celery, and nuts; mix lightly and refrigerate.

At serving time, spoon salad on lettuce. Garnish with avocado slices dipped in remaining lemon juice. Serves 4 to 6.

In order to have a salad which will appeal to the eye and to the appetite, it is necessary first of all that the ingredients should be of first quality.

Crab Collection

CRAB MEAT COCKTAIL

⅓ cup catsup

1 tablespoon lemon juice

2 teaspoons Worcestershire sauce

¼ teaspoon salt

⅛ teaspoon pepper

1 tablespoon prepared horseradish

¾ cup chopped celery

1 pound crab meat

1 medium-size avocado

For cocktail sauce; combine catsup, lemon juice, Worcestershire sauce, salt, pepper, and horseradish in a small bowl; reserve.

Place 2 tablespoons chopped celery into each of six individual salad bowls; top with 3 ounces of crab meat.

Peel and pit avocado; slice in half lengthwise. Cut each half into six lengthwise slices; place one slice on each side of the crab meat. Serve with cocktail sauce. Serves 6.

Serve this delightful salad in a glass bowl for a most attractive presentation. Serve with a wine such as a Rhine or a green Hungarian or a less dry wine such as a sweet Sauterne.

Crab Collection

CRAB MEAT AND CANTALOUPE SALAD

½ cup plain low-fat yogurt

¼ cup reduced-calorie mayonnaise

1 tablespoon chopped fresh parsley

1 tablespoon chopped fresh mint

¼ teaspoon sugar

2 teaspoons lemon juice

3 cups alfalfa sprouts

12 red leaf lettuce leaves

1 pound fresh lump crab meat

1 medium unpeeled cucumber, scored and sliced

1 cup sliced fresh strawberries

1 medium cantaloupe, peeled, seeded, and cut lengthwise into ¼-inch slices

Combine first six ingredients; stir well. Cover and chill.

Arrange ¾ cup alfalfa sprouts and three lettuce leaves on each of four serving plates. Spoon crab meat evenly over lettuce leaves; arrange cucumber and strawberries over alfalfa sprouts. Arrange cantaloupe slices evenly down center of each plate.

Serve salad with chilled yogurt mixture. Yield: 4 servings.

Nothing refreshes more on a warm day than melons ripe off the vine.

Recipe adapted from Cooking Light Magazine

PINEAPPLE CRAB SALAD

1 pound crab meat
½ cup diced celery
1 hard-cooked egg, diced
¼ cup green pepper
½ cup salad dressing
1 small can pineapple chunks

Combine ingredients, chill, and serve. Serves 4 to 6.

On a hot summer's evening, cool and refreshing pineapple crab salad is a perfect choice for that special dinner.

Crab Collection

GIANT CRAB MEAT SALAD

1 pound crab meat
2 stalks celery, chopped
1 sour pickle, chopped
2 tablespoons capers
2 teaspoons dry mustard
1½ teaspoon mixed parsley and tarragon, finely chopped

Mix all ingredients thoroughly and serve on lettuce. Serves 4 to 6.

Cut out the core of a lettuce head. Wash under cold water, drain, place in covered dish, put in refrigerator, and use the leaves as needed. The leaves will stay fresh and crisp.

Giant Food Stores, Landover, Maryland

CHESAPEAKE BAY CRAB SALAD

1 pound crab meat
¼ cup mayonnaise
1 teaspoon chopped pimiento
2 tablespoons Dijon mustard
1½ teaspoons Worcestershire sauce
½ teaspoon salt
¼ teaspoon hot pepper sauce
juice of 1 lemon
⅓ cup chopped celery
lettuce, lemon slices, and paprika

Remove cartilage from crab meat. In bowl, mix mayonnaise, pimiento, mustard, Worcestershire sauce, salt, hot pepper sauce, lemon juice, and celery. Blend well. Pour over crab meat and toss lightly but evenly. Refrigerate. Serve in bowl lined with lettuce leaves. Garnish with lemon slices and sprinkle with paprika. Serves 4 to 6.

According to an old Spanish proverb: "It takes four persons to make a salad—a spendthrift for the oil, a miser for the vinegar, a counselor for the salt, and a madman to stir them up.

Maryland Department of Seafood Marketing, Annapolis, Maryland

WEST COAST CRAB LOUIS SALAD

½ cup mayonnaise
½ cup chili sauce
2 tablespoons chopped green pepper
2 tablespoons choppped sweet pickle
1 tablespoon chopped onion
1 tablespoon lemon juice
1 pound lump crab meat
lettuce
2 tomatoes, quartered
2 green peppers, sliced
2 hard-cooked eggs, diced
pimiento strips

Combine mayonnaise, chili sauce, chopped green pepper, sweet pickle, onion, and lemon juice; blend well. Add crab meat, tossing lightly. Chill thoroughly.

At serving time, spoon salad onto lettuce. Garnish with tomatoes, green pepper slices, eggs, and pimiento. Serves 4 to 6.

The west coast has received credit for developing this wonderful recipe. Regardless of the type of crab meat you use, Dungeness or blue, it's always a delight.

Crab Collection

SURRY CRAB-STUFFED AVOCADOS

1 pound fresh crab meat
1 (11-ounce) can mandarin oranges, drained
¼ cup plus 1 tablespoon vegetable oil
½ cup sliced green onions with tops
2 tablespoons wine vinegar
½ teaspoon garlic salt
3 small avocados, peeled
2 tablespoons lemon juice
lettuce leaves

Combine fresh crab meat, mandarin oranges, oil, green onions, vinegar, and garlic salt; mix well.

Cut avocados in half lengthwise; remove seeds. Brush avocado halves with lemon juice and fill with crab meat mixture. Arrange avocado halves on lettuce leaves. Yield: 6 servings.

To the creative cook who likes to add a little flair to the menu, crab-stuffed avocados offer imaginative serving possibilities.

Crab Collection

MA BRUDVIG'S CRAB SALAD

1 cup mayonnaise

2 tablespoons chili sauce

3 tablespoons olive oil

1 tablespoon wine vinegar

2 tablespoons finely chopped onion

6 tablespoons cream

Worcestershire sauce

salt, pepper, cayenne

1 pound crab meat

tomatoes, lettuce, and sliced hard-boiled
    eggs to garnish

Blend together mayonnaise, chili sauce, olive oil, wine vinegar, onion, and cream. Season to taste with Worcestershire sauce, salt, pepper, and cayenne. Stir and chill until ready to serve. Add flaked crab meat to sauce and fold in gently. Place on lettuce and arrange with tomato quarters and sliced eggs. Serves 6.

Whatever the salad choice of the homemaker may be, the salad should be served on thoroughly chilled plates and with maximum eye appeal for one and all.

Frances Brudvig, Arlington, Virginia

POTOMAC RIVER CRAB SALAD

1 pound lump crab meat
½ cup celery, diced
1 hard-cooked egg, diced
¼ cup green pepper, diced
salt and pepper to taste
mayonnaise
paprika

Combine ingredients with enough mayonnaise to mix and sprinkle with paprika. (Pineapple chunks may be substituted for egg.) Serves 4 to 6.

Neptune himself would approve of the simplicity and pure flavor of this dish. On one of those steamy summer afternoons, serve this with a white wine for an impeccable brunch.

Keyser Brothers, Inc., Lottsburg, Virginia

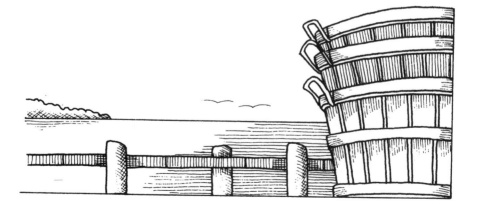

CRAB ARUNDEL

1 cup mayonnaise

¼ cup heavy cream

½ cup chili sauce

2 tablespoons chopped green olives

1 teaspoon prepared horseradish

1 teaspoon Worcestershire sauce

2 green onions, chopped fine

1 tablespoon lemon juice

1 pound fresh crab meat

crisp lettuce

chopped parsley or chives

1 tomato, quartered

1 egg, quartered

Prepare dressing by combining the first eight ingredients. Arrange the crab meat in a bed of crisp lettuce. Cover with dressing and garnish with the chopped parsley or chives. Arrange quartered tomatoes and quartered hard-cooked eggs around symmetrically. Serves 4.

The perfect dinner is perfect because of the attention given to every detail. The creative cook believes vegetables deserve more attention than they are often given.

Crab Collection

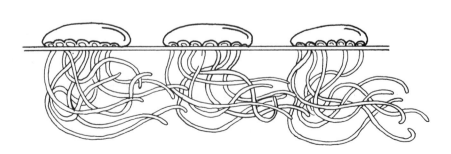

ARTICHOKE AND CRAB MEAT SALAD

1 cup diced cooked artichoke hearts
1 cup crab meat
½ cup heavy cream, whipped
1 cup mayonnaise
½ cup tomato catsup
½ teaspoon Worcestershire sauce
salt and pepper

Mix artichokes and crab meat and chill. Whip cream and combine with mayonnaise, catsup, Worcestershire sauce, salt, and pepper. Chill. When ready to serve, combine sauce with the artichoke and crab mixture. Serves 6.

Prepare this salad early in the day and it will be ready to serve for dinner.

Crab Collection

TOMATOES WITH CRAB MEAT DRESSING

1 pound crab meat
1 cup grated carrot
2 hard-cooked eggs, chopped
1 tablespoon chopped onion
1 cup mayonnaise
¼ cup lemon juice
1 teaspoon prepared mustard
1 teaspoon salt
1 teaspoon pepper
18 tomato slices
6 lettuce leaves

Remove any remaining shell or cartilage from crab meat. Combine carrot, egg, onion, and crab meat. Combine mayonnaise, lemon juice, mustard, salt, and pepper; mix thoroughly. Add mayonnaise mixture to crab mixture; toss lightly. Chill. Arrange three tomato slices on each lettuce leaf; sprinkle with salt. Top tomatoes with approximately ⅔ cup crab meat dressing. Serves 6.

Nothing sharpens the edge of appetities like home-grown tomatoes and fresh picked buttercrunch lettuce.

Crab Collection

ASPARAGUS CRAB SALAD

1 pound crab meat

6 to 8 spears cooked asparagus

½ zucchini, sliced and parboiled

6 to 8 carrot curls

2 tablespoons sliced ripe olives

lettuce

2 tablespoons each oil and white wine
vinegar

2 teaspoons diced pimiento

¼ teaspoon salt

¼ teaspoon dry mustard

⅛ teaspoon pepper

⅛ teaspoon tarragon

Arrange crab with vegetables and olives on six lettuce-lined salad plates. Combine remaining ingredients; drizzle over salads. Chill thoroughly. Serves 6.

Alaska king crab, known for its large size and delicate flavor, is caught in the icy waters off the coast of Alaska. The meat is carefully processed and sent to markets throughout the country. Try different types of crab meat to add variety to your favorite recipe.

Crab Collection

SEA ISLAND CRAB COCKTAIL

1 pound crab meat
lettuce
cocktail sauce
parsley
lemon wedges

Arrange lettuce in six cocktail glasses. Place crab meat on top; cover with cocktail sauce. Garnish with parsley and lemon wedges. Serves 6.

COCKTAIL SAUCE

¾ cup catsup
¼ cup lemon juice
½ teaspoon salt
6 drops Tabasco sauce
dash cayenne pepper
1 teaspoon Worcestershire sauce
horseradish

Combine all ingredients and chill.

This recipe is a classic in the true sense of the word.

Lewis Crab Factory, Inc., Brunswick, Georgia

Crab Cakes

JOE'S CRAB CAKES

1 pound crab meat
2 slices fresh bread, crusts removed
1 egg
1 tablespoon prepared mustard
2 tablespoons mayonnaise
1 teaspoon Worcestershire sauce
dash hot sauce
1 tablespoon minced fresh parsley
oil for frying

Cut bread into small cubes. Combine with other ingredients and form into cakes about 2 inches in diameter. Place on cookie sheet in refrigerator until firm. In ½-inch of oil, fry in heavy skillet until golden brown. Turn and brown other side. Yield: about 10 cakes.

Washington, DC fire fighter Joe O'Neil, "Chief of the Kitchen," says the main thing about cooking for firemen is cooking enough. So, you may as well double this recipe and, like any good cook, make enough to be held over.

The Washington Star, June 14, 1978

JUDY'S CRAB CAKES

1 pound freshly picked crab meat
1 egg
¼ cup finely chopped green pepper
2 tablespoons finely minced onion
1 tablespoon mayonnaise
1 teaspoon Old Bay Seafood Seasoning
2 tablespoons butter

In a bowl, beat egg slightly. Add remaining ingredients except butter and mix gently and thoroughly. Shape into cakes.

Melt 2 tablespoons butter in non-stick fry pan. Over medium heat, fry cakes until golden brown in each side. Serves 4.

This recipe for fresh picked crab is easily doubled for serving a group. The distinct flavor of the onions and green pepper bring out the natural sweet flavor of the crab meat.

Judy Hopkins, Dunkirk, Maryland

JAMES RIVER CRAB CAKES

½ teaspoon powdered mustard

1 teaspoon water

1 pound crab meat

3 egg yolks

2 tablespoons mayonnaise

5 teaspoons of bread crumbs

2 teaspoons lemon juice

dash cayenne

⅛ teaspoon ground mace

salt to taste

1 tablespoon cold water

flour

1 tablespoon butter

2 tablespoons salad oil

Mix the mustard with the water and let the mixture stand 5 minutes. Flake crab meat and remove any pieces of shell. Add the mustard, 2 of the egg yolks, mayonnaise, 5 teaspoons of bread crumbs, lemon juice, cayenne, mace, and salt to taste. Mix the ingredients well. Shape the mixture into eight cakes. Chill 30 minutes. Beat the remaining egg yolk with cold water. Roll the cakes in flour, dip them into the egg yolk and then roll them in fine dry bread crumbs. Heat the butter and the oil in a skillet, add the crab cakes, and brown both sides. Serves 4.

Serve with corn-on-the-cob and sliced tomato along with iced tea and a fresh sprig of mint.

Crab Collection

SOUTHERN CRAB CAKES

1 pound crab meat
1 cup seasoned bread crumbs
¼ cup melted butter
2 eggs, slightly beaten
1 carrot, scraped and grated
1½ teaspoons chopped parsley
2 teaspoons mayonnaise
1½ teaspoons Worcestershire sauce
1 teaspoon salt
¾ teaspoon dry mustard
¼ teaspoon pepper
1 egg, slightly beaten
2 tablespoons water
¾ cup dry bread crumbs
6 tablespoons melted butter

Combine first 11 ingredients; stir well. Shape into six patties (mixture will be slightly loose). Cover and chill mixture 1 hour.

Combine 1 egg and water, beat well. Dip patties in egg mixture; then dredge in ¾ cup bread crumbs. Saute crab cakes in butter, turning once, until golden brown. Drain on paper towels. Serves 6.

With their golden exterior and a creamy interior, it's easy to see why these cakes are so popular in the south.

Crab Collection

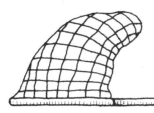

THOMAS POINT CRAB CAKES

¼ cup chopped celery
¼ cup chopped onion
4 tablespoons chopped green pepper
2 egg yolks
2 tablespoons mayonnaise
1 teaspoon dry mustard
dash each of hot sauce, seafood seasoning
lemon
1 pound fresh backfin crab meat
3 slices chopped white bread
⅓ cup cooking oil

Make sauce by mixing all ingredients except crab and bread, set aside. Mix crab and bread; fold gently into sauce and form into patties. Heat ⅓ cup cooking oil in a large heavy skillet over moderately high heat, add cakes and brown 3 to 4 minutes on each side. Drain well on paper towel. Serves 4 to 6.

The chopped white bread provides an edible holder for the crab cake and one that does not flatten its flavor. Enjoy.

Crab Collection

BALTIMORE CRAB CAKES

1 tablespoon mayonnaise

¼ teaspoon salt

1 egg

¼ teaspoon poultry seasoning

¼ teaspoon parsley flakes

1 tablespoon baking powder

2 tablespoons milk

2 slices of white bread

1 pound backfin crab meat

oil for frying

Combine mayonnaise, egg (beaten), salt, poultry seasoning, and parsley flakes. Add baking powder. Remove crust from bread, dice into small cubes, and moisten with milk. Add to mixture. Carefully remove cartilage (shells) from crab meat and gently fold in. Form cakes into small balls. Refrigerate for at least 30 minutes. Deep fry at 350 degrees until golden brown. Serves 4 to 6.

These cakes may be frozen after 30 minutes refrigeration, giving baking powder time to act.

Crab Collection

HANDY'S CRAB BURGERS

1 pound claw crab meat
1 cup mayonnaise
salt
2 tablespoons minced green pepper
¾ cup chopped celery
2 tablespoons minced onion
few drops Worcestershire sauce
few drops Tabasco
1 cup sharp cheddar cheese, cubed small
8 hamburger buns, split in halves
grated Parmesan cheese

Combine above ingredients, except hamburger buns and Parmesan cheese, in a bowl. Season to taste with salt and sauces; refrigerate until ready to serve.

Brown the split buns, spread with crab mixture, sprinkle with grated Parmesan, and broil until lightly browned and bubbly. Serves 8.

Eating crab is a piece of cake.

Mrs. John T. Handy, Crisfield, Maryland

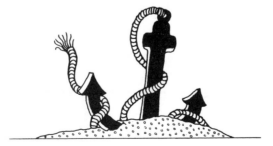

YARDLEY'S CRAB CAKES

1 pound lump crab meat
1 egg
2 slices bread
1 tablespoon chopped parsley
1 tablespoon prepared mustard
1 teaspoon Worcestershire sauce
salt and pepper
bacon fat for frying

Pull inside of bread into small pieces, soak well in beaten egg with mustard and seasonings; add crab meat (try not to break it). Form into cakes and cook until brown in very hot bacon fat. Makes 6 big cakes. Serves 3.

Just a walk out on a rickety pier, then sit by the window and order a beer, then order a crab cake—Yardley, I'm sure appreciates this simple pleasure.

Yardley, The Baltimore Sun, Baltimore, Maryland

GLORIA DAVIS' MARYLAND CRAB CAKES

2 eggs

2 slices white bread, cut into ½-inch pieces

1 pound crab meat

1 tablespoon mayonnaise

1 teaspoon Dijon mustard

1 teaspoon horseradish

parsley, minced

salt and pepper, to taste

1 tablespoon butter, for frying

4 soft rolls for serving

Mix together eggs and bread. Add remaining ingredients, except butter and rolls, and mold into six patties. Melt butter in frying pan over medium heat and fry crab cakes on both sides until golden brown. Serve on warmed rolls. Serves 4.

We give Gloria Davis thanks for these cakes. The best and most remarkable thing is that they are so perfect.

Crab Collection

HELEN AND JOHN'S CRAB CAKES

1 pound backfin crab meat

2 day-old hamburger buns

1 tablespoon parsley

almost ½ cup mayonnaise

a shake red pepper

corn flake crumbs

1 tablespoon Old Bay Seasoning

¼ teaspoon salt

1 tablespoon Worcestershire sauce

2 tablespoons water

1 tablespoon finely chopped onion

Go through crab meat to eliminate any shells. Rub hamburger rolls through hands until very fine and mix with crab meat. Mix together all other ingredients and add with crab meat. Divide mixed crab meat into eight separate piles on wax paper. Shape into cakes, then coat with corn flake crumbs. Fry in oil until brown on both sides. Drain on paper towels. (Alternative: Place crab cakes in shells and bake at 350 degrees for 45 minutes.) Serves 4.

These crab cakes are much better when eaten a day after they are mixed; this allows the seasonings to penetrate properly.

Helen and John Gordon, Lakeland, Florida

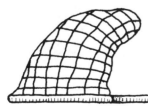

MARYLAND PAVILION CRAB CAKES

1 pound crab meat
2 eggs
2 tablespoons mayonnaise
1 tablespoon horseradish mustard
1 tablespoon chopped parsley
¼ teaspoon salt
⅛ teaspoon pepper
dash liquid hot-pepper sauce
crackers or cracker crumbs
oil for frying

In a bowl, combine crab meat, eggs, mayonnaise, horseradish mustard, chopped parsley, salt, pepper, and hot-pepper sauce. Mix lightly. Separate and form into 12 to 16 small cakes; do not pack firmly. Roll crackers into fine crumbs. Pat the cracker crumbs lightly onto the crab cakes. Heat oil to a depth of about ¼inch in a large skillet, or heat the oil in a deep fryer. Fry crab cakes until golden brown, turning once. Drain on paper toweling. Serves 6.

This recipe came from the Maryland Pavilion at the 1964-1965 New York World's Fair.

Crab Collection

MARYLAND LADY CRAB CAKES

1 pound crab meat
1 cup Italian seasoned bread crumbs
1 large egg (or 2 small)
¼ cup mayonnaise
½ teaspoon salt
¼ teaspoon black pepper
1 teaspoon Worcestershire sauce
1 teaspoon dry mustard
fat or oil for frying

Remove all cartilage from crab meat. In a bowl, mix bread crumbs, egg, mayonnaise, and seasonings. Add crab meat, and mix gently but thoroughly. Shape into six cakes.

Fry in hot fat (350 degrees) until browned, or pan fry in a little butter or oil until browned on both sides. Makes six crab cakes.

According to "Ye Maryland Chronicle" written for the Baltimore Sunday Sun in 1933, the Maryland crab was the main reason for Captain John Smith's visit to the Chesapeake Bay in 1607. Crab cakes were first eaten by Lord Baltimore in 1634.

Seafood Market Development Division, Maryland Department of Chesapeake Bay Affairs

DEAN'S CAKES

1 pound crab meat
1 tablespoon minced green pepper
red pepper to taste
black pepper to taste
mayonnaise
butter for frying

To the crab meat, add peppers and combine with enough mayonnaise to bind the crab meat into cakes. Fry until golden. Serves 4.

Crab meat is one of summer's most delightful culinary specialties. It can be prepared quickly, served hot or cold, and is ideal for the weight-watching mood of the sun-bathing months. This recipe is simple to prepare and is intended to feed four people. Dean says he got the recipe from a cab driver and so he passed it on to me. Thanks, Dean!

Dean Gore, Annandale, Virginia

BOOKBINDER'S CRAB CAKES

1 tablespoon green pepper
1 tablespoon minced onions
1 tablespoon celery
1 tablespoon pimiento
salt and pepper to taste
½ teaspoon thyme
1 teaspoon Worcestershire sauce
2 teaspoons butter
4 tablespoons flour
1 cup milk
1 pound crab meat
2 eggs, beaten
bread crumbs

Mix vegetables and seasonings. Cook in butter on low heat for 10 minutes. Add flour and stir to blend well. Add milk and crab and mix. Chill and form into cakes, dip into egg and then into bread crumbs, and fry. Serves 6.

Debbie recalls this recipe from growing up on the eastern shore of Maryland. Today she uses it when unexpected guests arrive, just as her Mom did. Thanks Mom!

Debbie Stromberg, Arlington, Virginia

SWISS CRAB MELT

2 English muffins
8 ounces crab meat
4 slices tomato
salt and pepper
⅓ cup finely chopped celery
1 teaspoon lemon juice
mayonnaise
4 slices Swiss cheese

Split English muffins, and broil until lightly browned; top each half with a fourth of the crab meat. Place a slice of tomato on each, and sprinkle with salt and pepper.

Combine celery, lemon juice, and enough mayonnaise to make a spreading consistency; spread over tomato slices. Top with cheese slices, and broil until cheese melts. Yields 2 to 4 servings.

Sandwich meals are always in demand, especially for busy days when time is limited. For a lunch that is both hot and hearty, accompany with a green garden salad.

Crab Collection

WORCESTER CRAB SANDWICH

1 cup crab meat

½ cup shredded cheese

½ cup chopped celery

2 tablespoons sweet pickle

2 tablespoons chopped onion

1 hard-cooked egg, chopped

3 tablespoons mayonnaise

½ teaspoon lemon juice

½ teaspoon horseradish

5 sliced tomatoes

5 slices bread

Combine all ingredients except the tomatoes and bread. Season to taste and spread on five slices of bread. Top with tomatoes. Grill until golden. Yields 5 serving.

You have prepared your entire meal well in advance, so relax and visit with your guests. There's nothing left to do but enjoy yourself.

Crab Collection

FETCHER ISLAND CRAB CUTLETS

3 tablespoons butter
5 tablespoons flour
1½ cups milk
salt and pepper
1 egg, beaten
dash celery salt
1 teaspoon grated onion
1 pound crab meat
mayonnaise
dry bread crumbs
2 tablespoons butter

Melt butter, blend in flour, add milk, and cook stirring constantly until thick. Add salt, pepper, beaten egg, celery salt, and onion and cook until very thick. Add crab meat to first mixture. Chill for several hours. Form into cakes or cut into small steak-shaped pieces, dip into flour, then spread generously on both sides with mayonnaise and roll in crumbs. Brown in hot butter. Serves 6.

Serve with creamed peas, catsup or cheese sauce, and wedges of lemon. This is a perfect main dish for a spring dinner.

Crab Collection

CRAB CAKE CLASSIC

1 package Old Bay Original Recipe Crab
  Cake Classic™
1 pound crab meat
½ cup mayonnaise

Mix contents of package with mayonnaise, then combine mixture with crab meat, gently but thoroughly. Shape into six cakes, then fry or broil until golden. For best results, do not make up more than 3 hours in advance. May be frozen before or after cooking. Yields 6 servings.

The Baltimore Spice Company says, "At last, now you can savor the bay at home. This original Maryland recipe crab cake mix turns ordinary crab meat into a Chesapeake Bay classic, easily and conveniently."

The Baltimore Spice Co., Baltimore, Maryland

JAKE'S CRAB CAKES

1 pound crab meat
⅔ cup plain bread crumbs
1 egg
1½ tablespoons mayonnaise
1 teaspoon dry mustard
⅓ teaspoon black pepper
1 teaspoon salt
salad oil for sauteing

Pick over crab meat. Combine all ingredients and shape into ten crab cakes. Saute in oil until brown. Serves 5.

In this recipe, nothing is added that might interfere with the perfect, natural sweetness of the crab meat.

Crab Collection

T. L.'S CRAB CAKES

1 pound crab meat
1 egg yolk
1½ teaspoons salt
1 teaspoon dry mustard
2 teaspoons Worcestershire sauce
2 tablespoons mayonnaise
1 tablespoon chopped parsley
1½ teaspoons paprika
1 teaspoon butter, melted
bread crumbs

Pick over crab meat to remove shells. Add all other ingredients except bread crumbs and toss lightly. Shape into cakes, roll in bread crumbs and fry quickly in hot fat. Makes 6 to 8 cakes.

Crab cakes are wonderful when served with traditional accompaniments such as french fries, coleslaw, beer, and lemon wedges. Some say spare the crab cake and skip the lemon juice. We let you be the judge.

Crab Collection

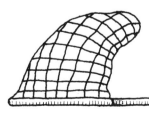

ALTHEA'S CRAB MEAT CAKES

1 pound crab meat

½ teaspoon salt

¼ teaspoon black pepper

2 teaspoons onion juice

2 teaspoons parsley flakes

2 eggs, beaten

2 teaspoons dry mustard

2 slices dry wheat bread made into crumbs

1 tablespoon baking powder

4 tablespoons butter, softened slightly

¼ teaspoon seafood seasoning

Combine all ingredients and shape into cakes. Pan fry in butter until browned on both sides. Serves 4.

Family and guests will enjoy these delicious flavors. Complete your meal with a crisp salad or green beans.

Althea Cheseldine, District Heights, Maryland

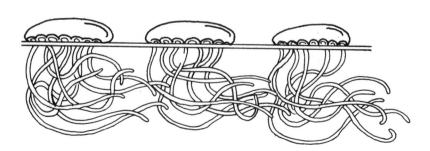

OLD BAY CRAB CAKES

2 slices bread, crusts removed
milk
1 pound crab meat
1 egg, beaten
¼ teaspoon salt
1 teaspoon Old Bay Seasoning
1 tablespoon baking powder
1 tablespoon chopped parsley
1 tablespoon Worcestershire sauce
1 tablespoon mayonnaise
oil for frying

Break bread in small pieces and moisten with milk; combine with remaining ingredients. Shape into patties. Fry quickly in 3 or 4 tablespoons hot oil until brown. Serves 6.

When The Baltimore Spice Company left the crab cake recipe off of the Old Bay Seafood Seasoning can, its switch boards lit up with callers wanting to know why. Here it is so it's always close at hand.

The Baltimore Spice Co., Baltimore, Maryland

HOT CRAB SANDWICHES

1 tablespoon chopped sweet pickle
1 tablespoon chopped onion
1 tablespoon chopped celery
3 tablespoons mayonnaise
½ teaspoon salt
dash pepper
1 pound crab meat
2 eggs, beaten
½ cup milk
¼ teaspoon salt
12 slices white bread

Combine pickle, onion, celery, mayonnaise, seasonings, and crab meat. Combine egg, milk, and salt. Dip one side of each slice of bread in egg mixture. Place bread in a heavy frying pan which contains about ⅛ inch of fat, hot but not smoking. Fry at moderate heat until brown on one side. Drain on absorbent paper. Spread plain side of 6 slices of bread with crab mixture; cover with remaining 6 slices of bread. Place on a well-greased cookie sheet, 15½ x 12 inches. Heat in a moderate oven, 350 degrees for 5 to 8 minutes or until heated through. Serves 6.

Ice-cold beer or ale is a good partner for these sandwiches, or try an India pale ale for an interesting change of pace.

Crab Collection

CHESAPEAKE CRAB CAKES

12 pounds crab meat, hand picked
2 soft-ball sized onions, chopped fine
¼ cup cayenne pepper
1 bunch celery, chopped fine
1 bunch parsley, chopped fine
26 eggs (beaten)
small bottle Tabasco sauce
1 squeezed lemon

Cook all water out of onions and celery and add to crab. Mix in uncooked parsley. Add remainder of ingredients and mix well. Deep fry 3-ounce patties at 350 degrees until they float. Serve hot. Makes about 100 servings.

Crabs cooked using the above recipe are really a delight—you can eat them in the morning and all through the night.

Chesapeake Crab House, Arlington, Virginia

MARYLAND CRAB CAKES

4 slices white bread

1 cup milk

2 pounds crab meat

2 tablespoons mayonnaise

2 teaspoons prepared mustard

2 teaspoons seafood seasoning

2 teaspoons baking powder

2 tablespoons chopped parsley

½ teaspoon Worcestershire sauce

juice of ½ lemon

salt and pepper

2 eggs, beaten

3 to 4 tablespoons shortening (for frying)

Put bread in bowl, pour milk over it and soak 15 minutes. Squeeze bread fairly dry in your fist, transfer it to a large bowl and break it into crumbs with two forks.

Add crab meat, mayonnaise, mustard, seafood seasoning, baking powder and parsley and stir until well mixed. Sprinkle with Worcestershire sauce, lemon juice, salt and pepper, and stir and taste for seasoning. Stir in beaten eggs. Crab cake mixture can be prepared up to 4 hours ahead and refrigerated.

To finish, divide mixture into 16 parts and shape into cakes about ½-inch thick. (Work gently so cakes are light.) In a large frying pan heat half the shortening and fry half the cakes over brisk heat until golden, about 2 minutes. Turn and brown the other side. Fry remaining cakes in remaining shortening and serve as soon as possible. Yield: 16 servings.

Traditionally made with meat from the east coast blue crab, crab cakes are great when prepared with any type of crab meat.

Washington Post Newspaper, Washington, DC

FOX ISLAND CRAB POTATO CAKES

1 pound claw crab meat
1 cup mashed potatoes
1 egg, beaten
½ teaspoon salt
dash pepper
dash onion salt

Combine all ingredients. Shape into 12 cakes. Place cakes in a heavy frying pan which contains about ⅛ inch of fat, hot but not smoking. Fry at moderate heat. When cakes are brown on one side, turn carefully and brown on the other side. Cooking time, approximately 5 to 8 minutes. Drain on absorbent paper. Serves 6.

Full-bodied white wine is in order; try a Chardonnay or Pinot Blanc from California.

Fish and Wildlife Series, U.S. Department of the Interior

COATED CRAB CAKES EXPRESSO

1 pound crab meat
salt and pepper to taste
bacon fat for frying
1 envelope barbecue mix for chicken
2 teaspoons seafood seasoning
¼ cup self-rising flour

Mix crab meat, salt, and pepper together and pat mixture into cakes. Mix flour, barbecue mix and seafood seasoning together. Coat crab cakes with flour mixture and fry in bacon fat until brown. Serves 8.

Tea, whether fresh or iced, is the time-honored drink to have with this meal. Well-chilled Chinese beer would also be very satisfying. This recipe was featured in "Martha's Cooking Seafood Cook Book."

Martha Drummond Curry, Reedville, Virginia

OYSTER HOUSE RD. CRAB CAKES

1½ slices white bread, crust removed
and diced

⅓ cup milk

1 pound crab meat

1 teaspoon fresh parsley, minced

1 teaspoon onion, minced

2 tablespoons mayonnaise

½ teaspoon Worcestershire sauce

½ teaspoon salt

freshly ground pepper

cayenne pepper

4 tablespoons butter

Soak bread pieces in milk for a few minutes. Add crab meat, parsley, onion, mayonnaise and Worcestershire sauce. Add salt and pepper to taste. Mix well, making sure crab meat is well integrated with other ingredients. Shape mixture into eight patties, each about 1 inch thick. Place patties on a flat pan and chill in the refrigerator for at least an hour.

Melt butter in a large, heavy skillet until gently sizzling. Cook chilled crab cakes about 4 to 5 minutes on each side, browning them well. Serve immediately. Serves 4.

We sometimes add a bare pinch of cayenne to point up the fine sweetness of the crab flavor.

Crab Collection

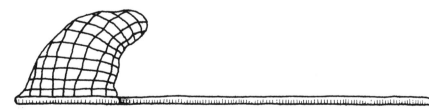

VIRGINIA BATTER CRAB CAKES

1 heel of bread

1 pound crab meat

2 tablespoons butter, melted

1 tablespoon minced fresh parsley

2 eggs, slightly beaten

2 teaspoons mayonnaise

2 teaspoons mustard

flour

fat or oil for frying

lemon wedges as garnish

Break bread into crab meat and toss lightly. Mix other ingredients and lightly fold into crab mixture. Shape into patties with a fork and spoon. Place on floured platter and dust tops with flour. Brown quickly on each side in small amount of fat or oil. Cover and steam cook for 3 minutes. Drain on paper towel. Serves 6. Note: Backfin crab meat is best for this recipe.

Among crustaceans, brave and bold—that succulent (crab) meat, oh so sweet, is worth its weight in gold.

Annie Hendricks, Alexandria, Virginia

CRAB CAKES MARIA

1 egg

2 tablespoons mayonnaise

½ teaspoon Dijon mustard

⅛ teaspoon ground hot red pepper (cayenne)

⅛ teaspoon hot pepper sauce

½ teaspoon salt

½ teaspoon ground white pepper

1 pound fresh lump or backfin crab meat

3 tablespoons finely chopped fresh parsley

1 to 2 tablespoons crumbs made from bread or unsalted soda crackers

flour

vegetable oil for deep frying

1 lemon cut into wedges

tartar sauce

In a deep bowl, beat the egg lightly with a wire whisk. Add the mayonnaise, mustard, red pepper, hot pepper sauce, salt, and white pepper and whisk until the mixture is smooth. Then add the crab meat, parsley, and crumbs, and very gently toss together with a fork. Try not to break up the crab meat. Leave lumps as large as possible. Divide the mixture into eight equal portions, and shape each of these into a ball about 2 inches in diameter. Roll lightly in flour. Wrap in waxed paper, and chill the cakes for 30 minutes. Deep-fry the crab cakes at 375 degrees until golden brown. Serve with lemon wedges and tartar sauce. Serves 4.

Serve at once, accompanied by tartar sauce along with the beverage of your choice. You will find this to be a jewel of a recipe.

Crab Collection

RAINBOW GIRLS CRAB FLUFF

1 pound crab meat

1 egg, slightly beaten

1 tablespoon parsley flakes

1½ teaspoons Old Bay Seasoning

10 saltine crackers

2 tablespoons mayonnaise

2 tablespoons mustard

oil for frying

Batter:

1 egg

1 cup self-rising flour

1½ tablespoons parsley flakes

milk

Mix crab meat, egg, parsley, and Old Bay together. Roll saltines with rolling pin to make crumbs. Add crumbs, mustard, and mayonnaise to crab mixture. Mix thoroughly. Shape into crab cakes. Make batter.

To make batter, whip egg with a spoon; add flour, parsley flakes, and milk to make batter like pancakes. Mix. Heat oil in fry pan or deep fryer enough to cover cakes. Dip cakes in batter. Fry until golden brown. Serves 4 to 6.

This recipe came from a cookbook put out by "Maryland Rainbow Girls," and was submitted by Al and Frances Drechsler of Fort Washington, Maryland

Maryland Rainbow Girls Cookbook

FANCY CRAB CAKES

1 pound backfin crab meat
2½ tablespoons butter
2 tablespoons flour
1 cup milk
3 tablespoons dry white wine
½ teaspoon dry mustard
¼ teaspoon white pepper
1 scallion, finely chopped
parsley, finely chopped
green pepper strip, chopped
1 egg, beaten
salt

Make a white sauce with butter and flour; then add milk, wine, mustard, pepper, and salt. Mix with crab and other ingredients. Form into large cakes and fry until golden. Serves 4.

Crab cakes cooked are a wonderful sight, you can eat them in the morning and all through the night—never have to worry about ever getting fat, you cook a batch and try them, and that will settle that.

Crab Collection

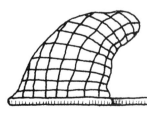

LUNCH MOUTH DUNGENESS CRABWICH

1 cup Dungeness crab meat

¼ cup sour cream

¼ cup mayonnaise

a few grains garlic salt

¼ teaspoon dill seed

¼ teaspoon paprika

1 teaspoon lemon juice

buttered bread

Combine first seven ingredients well. Spread big slices of buttered Russian rye bread with mixture for hearty appetites. Or, for open-faced luncheon treats, spread on regular rye, thin slices of pumpernickel or white bread cut into fancy shapes. Yields 1½ cups of crabwich mix.

A crab in every pot, a Dungeness dish for any meal.

Oregon Department of Agriculture, Salem, Oregon

Soft Shell Crab

SOFT SHELL CRABS, ROSE HAVEN

6 soft shell crabs, cleaned
1 cup all-purpose flour
6 tablespoons butter
2 cloves garlic, sliced in half
2 tablespoons lemon juice
¼ cup dry white wine
dash Tabasco sauce
1 teaspoon Worcestershire
dash of salt
dash of ground black pepper
2 tablespoons chopped parsley

Rinse the cleaned crabs and drain well. Place the flour in a plastic bag and dip the crabs, one at a time, into the flour until they are well coated.

Heat 2½ tablespoons butter in a large skillet. Saute 3 crabs at a time in hot butter for 2 to 2½ minutes or until golden; turn and repeat on other side. Remove crabs and keep warm in the oven; add another 2½ tablespoons butter and saute remaining crabs.

Discard butter but do not clean pan. Melt remaining tablespoon butter in pan. Add the garlic and lemon juice. Stir to remove browned bits from pan.

Add the wine, Tabasco, Worcestershire sauce, salt, and pepper to the pan. Cook for 2 minutes. Strain over crabs. Sprinkle with chopped parsley. Serves 3.

Soft shell crab season begins when the locust trees bloom in late May, and continues all summer long.

Crab Collection

VIRGINIA FRIED SOFT SHELL CRABS

12 soft crabs

¼ cup milk

¾ cup flour

2 eggs, beaten

2 teaspoons salt

¾ cup dry bread crumbs

Dress fresh crabs or thaw frozen crabs. Rinse in cold water; drain. Combine eggs, milk and salt. Combine flour and crumbs. Dip crabs in egg mixture and roll in flour/crumb mixture. For heavier breading, let crabs sit several minutes and repeat dipping-rolling procedure. Additional spices, such as cayenne pepper and garlic, may also be added.

Place crabs in a heavy frying pan which contains ⅛ to ¼ inch of fat, hot but not smoking. Fry at moderate heat. When crabs are brown on one side, turn carefully and brown the other side. Cooking time is approximately 8 to 10 minutes. Drain on absorbent paper. Serves 6.

If you prefer, you can fry the crabs in a basket in deep fat at 375 degrees for 3 to 4 minutes or until brown. Drain on absorbent paper.

Virginia Institute of Marine Sciences, Gloucester Point, Virginia

FRIED SOFT SHELL CRABS WITH BEER BATTER

¾ cup unbleached white flour
½ teaspoon salt
1 egg
1 teaspoon fresh ginger, minced
¾ cup beer (any kind but light)
12 fresh medium soft shell crabs
corn, safflower, or soy oil for frying

In a small mixing bowl, combine flour, salt, egg, and ginger and mix well. Add beer, mix, and let batter stand at room temperature for 2 to 3 hours. Using a wok or heavy skillet at least 10 inches in diameter, add the cooking oil and heat to 375 degrees. Dip crabs in batter and fry three crabs at once, dropping them into the oil one at a time. With tongs or slotted spoon, remove crabs and drain them on paper towels. Serves 4.

Serve crabs while still warm. Serve them plain or on home made egg bread as a sandwich with tartar or hot sauce.

Bethann Thornburg, The Washington Post, August 8, 1982

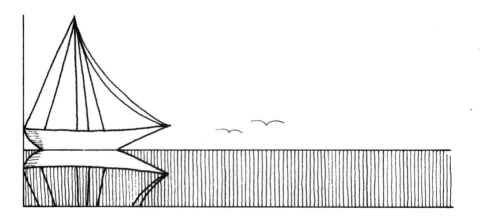

SOFT SHELL CRABS LINDO

6 soft shell crabs

2 cups milk

¼ teaspoon salt

¼ teaspoon pepper

oil

1 cup flour

½ teaspoon salt

¼ teaspoon black pepper

¼ teaspoon cayenne

Soak the crabs for 30 minutes in the milk to which you have added the salt and pepper. Rub the milk carefully into the crabs. Mix the flour, salt, pepper, and cayenne. Thoroughly coat the crabs and fry in hot fat until golden brown. Serves 6.

Serve hot with your favorite sauce such as tartar or a nice, hot sauce. Pour yourself a pint of Wild Goose Beer, ah!

Crab Collection

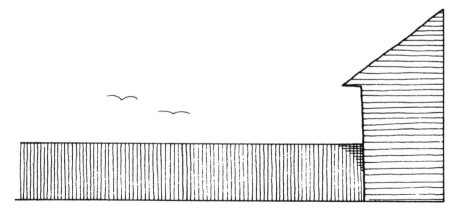

FRIED SOFT SHELL CRABS

6 soft crabs
1½ cups milk
½ teaspoon pepper
2 teaspoons salt
½ cup flour
shortening for frying
tartar sauce

Wash cleaned soft shell crabs. Dry well. Soak in milk seasoned with salt and pepper for 15 minutes; roll in flour. Heat shortening and fry crabs until crisp and brown. Drain on absorbent paper. Serve with tartar sauce or in sandwich. Serves 3.

Handle soft crabs delicately so that their natural flavor is allowed to dominate.

Crab Collection

FRIED SOFT SHELL CRABS

12 cleaned soft crabs
salt and pepper
flour
butter for frying

Dry crabs with paper towel. Sprinkle with salt and pepper. Lightly coat with flour. Cook crabs in fry pan, in just enough fat to prevent sticking, until browned; about 5 minutes on each side. Makes 6 servings.

If desired, crabs may be deep fried at 375 degrees for 2 to 3 minutes or until browned.

Maryland Department of Chesapeake Bay Affairs

SOFT SHELL CRABS WITH TARRAGON SAUCE

4 small or 3 large soft shell crabs, cleaned
flour for dredging
salt and pepper to taste
oil for frying
2 tablespoons butter
1 teaspoon finely chopped shallots
½ teaspoon vinegar
¼ cup white wine
2 branches fresh tarrragon, finely chopped
   (½ teaspoon dried)
2 fresh sage leaves, finely chopped
   (pinch dried)
2 fresh basil lesaves, finely chopped
   (¼ teaspoon dried)
2 fresh oregano leaves, chopped (¼
   teaspoon dried)

Combine flour, salt and pepper and coat crabs with mixture, shaking off excess. Heat oil in a skillet, add crabs and saute until golden. Drain and keep warm. Pour off oil from skillet. Add butter, shallots, vinegar and wine and beat with a wire whisk over low heat until mixture becomes creamy. Stir in tarragon, sage, basil, and oregano. Pour sauce over crabs and serve immediately. Serves 1.

This sauce can also be served on shrimp or light fish such as lemon sole or turbot. For this use, saute one clove garlic, finely chopped, in the skillet after discarding oil but before adding butter.

Crab Collection

SOFT SHELL CRABS, PECAN MONTELEONE

4 soft shell crabs, cut in quarters
seasoned flour
6 tablespoons butter
1 tablespoon finely chopped green onion
1 tablespoon chopped parsley
½ cup absinthe liqueur
3 egg yolks, beaten
½ cup cream
salt and pepper
16 tomato slices
16 toasted bread rounds
½ cup chopped pecans
dash cayenne pepper

Rinse crabs and dry with paper towel. Cut each crab into four parts. Toss crabs very lightly in seasoned flour. Melt butter in heavy skillet; when hot, put in crabs, shell side down. Reduce heat and saute crabs until brown. Turn crabs and brown on other side. When brown all over, remove to hot platter and keep warm.

Add 1 tablespoon of finely chopped onion and parsley to butter remaining in the skillet. Add ½ cup absinthe and simmer for 5 minutes. Have ready the yolks of three eggs beaten together with ½ cup of cream. Add this to absinthe broth, being careful not to let the broth boil after the egg mixture has been added. Salt and pepper to taste.

To serve, place tomato slices on toasted bread round, top with ¼ piece of soft shell crab, spoon over absinthe sauce, and sprinkle with chopped pecans and cayenne pepper. Yield: 16 hors d'oeuvres or 4 main course meals.

Chef Joseph Green was a double winner in the third annual crab cooking olympics in San Francisco. I saw the article and treasure this recipe.

Chef Joseph Green, Southern Living Magazine

BAKED SOFT SHELL CRABS

12 soft crabs

¼ cup milk

¾ cup flour

2 eggs, beaten

2 teaspoons salt

¾ cup dry bread crumbs

Dress fresh crabs or thaw frozen crabs. Rinse in cold water; drain. Combine eggs, milk and salt. Combine flour and crumbs. Dip crabs in egg mixture and roll in flour/crumb mixture. For heavier breading, let crabs sit several minutes and repeat dipping-rolling procedure. Place crabs in a greased baking pan. Put a little butter on each crab and place the pan in a hot oven (400 degrees) for about 8 minutes. Serves 6.

Once you've cleaned the soft crab, you're ready to enjoy this gourmet delight. The most common preparation technique is fried, but this baked recipe will give equally tasty results.

Virginia Institute of Marine Sciences, Gloucester Point, Virginia

SAUTEED SOFT SHELL CRABS

6 soft shell crabs, cleaned and rinsed
unbleached white flour for dredging
¼ cup safflower oil
2 tablespoons butter
¼ teaspoon hot pepper oil
1 tablespoon soy sauce
1 teaspoon minced fresh ginger root
2 scallions, cut into 1-inch lengths
lemon wedges for garnish

Dredge each crab in flour, shake off excess and set aside. In a skillet large enough to accommodate all six crabs, heat oil and butter over medium heat. Add hot oil, soy sauce, ginger, scallions and saute for 2 minutes. Turn heat up and add crabs. Saute 5 minutes or until crisp and reddish brown on both sides.

Place crabs and scallions on a serving platter. Turn heat up and let liquids in skillet come to a boil. Pour sauce over crabs and scallions. Serves 2.

Serve this dish while still hot. Garnish with lemon wedges. Steamed rice is a good accompaniment with the sauce spooned onto the rice by each diner.

Bethann Thornburg, The Washington Post, June 26, 1986

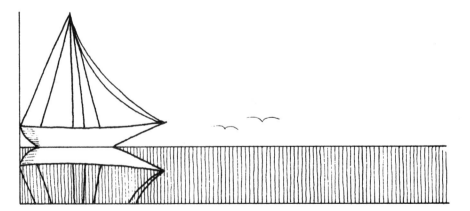

SAUTEED SOFT SHELL CRABS

12 soft crabs, cleaned
salt and pepper
flour
6 tablespoons butter
2 tablespoons oil

Wash crabs and remove excess water. Season with salt and pepper and dip in flour. Heat butter and oil in skillet. Cook about 4 minutes per side until delicately browned and crisp. Serves 6.

If the mention of crab makes your mouth water, this is one recipe you're sure to enjoy.

Virginia Institute of Marine Sciences, Gloucester Point, Virginia

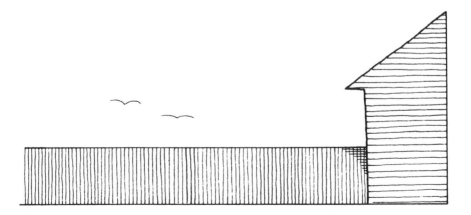

SOFT CRABS MIA

8 soft crabs, cleaned
¼ cup soy sauce
1½ cups white wine
⅓ cup olive oil
5 or 6 drops hot sauce
2 minced garlic cloves

Mix together all ingredients except crabs in a shallow baking dish. Add crabs and cover. Marinate for ½ hour.

Place crabs on a hot grill. Cook for 15 minutes on each side, basting and turning often. To decrease cooking time, cover grill with a large lid to help circulate the heat evenly.

Crabs are cooked when red, firm, and slightly crisp, but still moist. Serves 4.

The soft shell crab industry began during the 1870's in Crisfield, Maryland. The average annual production of soft crabs in the United States exceeds 2.6 million pounds, with the majority coming from the Chesapeake Bay.

Clare G. Vanerbeek, National Fisherman, August 1983

SOFT SHELL CRABS WITH BLACK BEAN SAUCE

8 soft shell crabs

flour

4 tablespoons butter

1 cup sake

4 green onions, minced

2 cloves garlic, minced or crushed

2 tablespoons fermented black beans, rinsed and chopped

Pat the crabs dry and dredge lightly in flour. Shake off excess. In a large skillet, melt 2 tablespoons of the butter over medium-high heat. Place 4 crabs in skillet, back-side down, and cook until lightly browned, about 2 minutes. Turn and cook until brown on the other side. Remove to a heated platter and keep warm in a low oven. Cook remaining crabs in remaining 2 tablespoons butter in the same way.

Increase heat to high. Pour the sake into the skillet and bring to boil, using a wooden spoon to scrape any browned bits out of the pan. Add the green onions and garlic and boil 1 minute until onions are limp. Add the black beans and boil 1 minute longer, stirring constantly. Spoon sauce over crabs and serve. Serves 4.

Sake is a sweet Japanese wine frequently served heated with meals. It is available in most liquor stores. If unavailable, substitute white wine, vermouth, or dry sherry.

Capital Newspaper, Annapolis, Maryland

SOFT CRAB LE CANARD

8 soft shell crabs

1 cup white wine

2 lemons

3 tablespoons butter

fresh chopped parsley

½ pound crab meat

2 tablespoons black beans, mashed

2 vine-ripened tomatoes

lemon slices for garnish

Saute soft crabs in wine, lemon juice, and butter for about 5 minutes on each side. Heat the crab meat until warm in same pan. Place crab meat in mounds into the cavity of the soft crabs. Garnish with black beans, vine-ripened tomatoes, and lemon slices. Serves 4.

Executive Chef Damien Heaney takes great pride in his crab dishes. His preparation of soft crabs is one of the best I have tasted. I think you will agree.

Le Canard Restaurant, Vienna, Virginia

GRILLED SOFT SHELL CRABS

12 soft shell crabs
seafood marinade (see below)

Liberally baste bottom side of crabs with marinade and care fully place, bottom-side down, on barbecue grill. Grill over slow fire, at least 12 inches from coals, for 5 minutes. Liberally baste top of crabs with marinade, turn carefully, and grill 5 minutes more. Serves 6.

SEAFOOD MARINADE

1 cup salad oil
2 tablespoons white vinegar
1 teaspoon salt
¼ teaspoon tarragon leaves
1 teaspoon lemon and pepper seasoning
1 teaspoon lemon juice
⅛ teaspoon garlic powder

Mix ingredients together. Let stand several hours at room temperature to let flavors blend before using. Makes 1 cup marinade.

The delicacy of the tender crabs and the light sauce calls for an equally delicate white wine. Hint—be sure it's well chilled.

Crab Collection

SOFT SHELL CRABS WITH PINE NUTS

12 soft shell crabs

flour

2 to 4 ounces butter

1 teaspoon peanut oil

course salt

2 to 4 small cloves garlic, chopped

¼ to ½ cup pine nuts

lemon wedges

Pat crabs dry with paper towels. Flour both sides of crab. Heat the butter and oil in the skillet until hot and foamy. Use medium heat. Saute shell side down first for 2 minutes. Shake skillet across burner if crabs stick. Salt lightly, then turn carefully with a spatula. Add the garlic and pine nuts. Use a spoon to coat nuts and garlic with butter sauce. Cook crabs 2 minutes more, adjusting heat if necessary. Spoon on sauce. Serve on hot plates with lemon wedges. Serves 4.

Pine nuts are not just for pesto, they give the soft crab an earthy flavor and make this meal an incomparable delight.

Crab Collection

SPICY STUFFED SOFT SHELLS

6 jumbo soft crabs

1 pound backfin lump crab meat

12 Ritz crackers (finely crushed)

1½ tablespoons Old Bay Seafood Seasoning

¼ teaspoon salt

¼ teaspoon pepper

1 tablespoon mustard

2 tablespoons mayonnaise

2 egg whites (lightly beaten)

flour to coat soft crabs

peanut oil for frying

lettuce, lemon and tomato wedges for garnish

Toss lump crab meat with cracker crumbs, Old Bay, salt, and pepper. Mix together mustard, mayonnaise, and egg whites. Add to crab meat and mix lightly.

Stuff soft crab cavity with mixture. Pile high enough to make a mound in center of soft crab. Shape with hands. Coat with flour. Brown on back first in about an inch of oil in electric fry pan at 375 degrees. Turn and brown on top side. Remove from oil with large slotted spoon. Drain on paper towels. Serve on lettuce leaf. Garnish with lemon and tomato wedges. Serves 6.

One of the finer pleasures of the late spring, early summer season is soft shell crabs, "softies." They can be prepared in a number of appetizing ways. Laura's unique method is one you will try again and again.

Laura Somers, Crisfield, Maryland

WYE ISLAND SOFT CRABS

½ cup butter, melted
1 teaspoon olive oil
¼ cup minced fresh basil leaves
4 tablespoons minced fresh parsley
¼ teaspoon cayenne pepper
24 soft shell crabs
¾ cup sliced almonds
basil leaves for garnish

Make basil butter: Blend together the butter, oil, basil, parsley, and cayenne. Set aside.

Grill the crabs: Brush the crabs with some of the basil butter. Place them directly on the prepared grill or thread them onto skewers. Grill for about 3 minutes on each side, until they turn a reddish color. Be sure that the crabs are cooked through, but do not overcook them. Brush them with more basil butter and sprinkle with the almonds. Serve immediately, garnish with basil leaves. Serves 8.

The delicacy of the tender crabs and the light sauce call for a delicate Chardonnay.

Crab Collection

Deviled Crab

DEVILLED DUNGENESS CRAB LEGS

¼ cup dry mustard
½ cup white wine
½ cup oyster sauce
bread crumbs
filberts finely chopped
25 ounces Dungeness crab legs
fat for frying
flour for dredging

SEASONED SAUCE

¼ cup dry mustard
½ cup white wine
½ cup oyster sauce
¼ cup ketchup

GARNISH

lemon wedges
filberts chopped
toasted sesame seeds

Combine mustard, white wine, and oyster sauce. Combine bread crumbs and filberts. Dredge Dungeness crab legs in flour, dip in mustard mixture, and roll in crumb and filbert mixture. Fry in oil at 360 degrees until browned. Can be served hot or cold with sauce for dipping. Garnish with lemon wedges, filberts, and toasted sesame seeds. Serves 25 as hos d'oeuvres or 6 for main course.

The Dungeness crab industry is more than just another fish story.

Carl Karaust, Silver Garden Restaurant, Portland, Oregon

MARTHA'S FRIED DEVILED HARD CRABS

8 medium-sized hard crabs, cleaned
1 cup self-rising flour
1 egg
dash Tabasco sauce
½ teaspoon salt
½ cup warm water
1 teaspoon mustard
3 teaspoons seafood seasoning
2 cups cooking oil

Mix flour, egg, Tabasco sauce, salt, water, mustard, and seafood seasoning together. Dip cleaned crabs in mixture and fry in hot oil in a frying pan until brown. Drain and serve. Serves 2.

You will find this dish hot, messy, and oh, so good. I adapted the recipe from Martha's Cooking Seafood Cookbook.

Martha Drummond Curry, Reedsville, Virginia

WYE RIVER DEVILED CRAB

1 cup chopped celery

2 small onions, chopped

1 teaspoon winter savory

½ teaspoon salt

½ teaspoon pepper

¼ cup melted butter

2 cups diced bread

1 egg, beaten

1 pound crab meat

Saute celery, onion, winter savory, salt, and pepper in melted butter until the vegetables are tender. Remove sauteed vegetables from heat, and stir in bread and egg. Return to low heat. Add crab meat, stirring lightly; cook 1 minute.

Spoon mixture into lightly buttered crab shells or ramekins, dividing mixture evenly. Place crab shells on cookie sheet. Bake at 350 degrees for 20 minutes or until light brown. Serves 6.

This savory version of deviled crab is one of the best we've tried; it doesn't cover up the flavor of the crab.

Crab Collection

JONES POINT DEVILED CRAB

1 small red onion, diced

¼ pound butter

½ pound claw crab meat

½ pound special crab meat

1 cup toasted bread crumbs

1 egg, beaten

2 tablespoons sherry

1 tablespoon Dijon mustard

1 pinch fresh parsley, chopped

1 teaspoon Worcestershire sauce

juice of 1 lemon

dash of pepper

paprika

Saute onion in butter until translucent, then transfer to large mixing bowl. Add crab meat, bread crumbs, egg, sherry, mustard, parsley, Worcestershire sauce, lemon juice, and pepper. Mix well. Fill eight crab shells or small souffle dishes with mixture; baste with butter remaining in saute pan. Sprinkle with paprika, then bake at 400 degrees for 20 to 25 minutes. Serves 8.

Round-out the flavors and color of this dish by serving accompaniments such as a tossed green salad, buttered corn, and hot rolls.

Crab Collection

OLD TOWN DEVILED CRAB

5 tablespoons butter

2 tablespoons flour

1 teaspoon dry mustard

1 cup milk

2 teaspoons lemon juice

1 tablespoon minced parsley

1 pound crab meat

½ cup soft bread crumbs

Make a white sauce with 3 tablespoons of the butter, flour, mustard, and milk; stir in lemon juice and parsley. Fold in crab. Spoon into six ceramic crab shells or similar utensils. Mix bread crumbs with remaining 2 tablespoons butter (melted) and sprinkle over crab mixture.

Before serving, bake in a preheated 400-degree oven until hot and topping is lightly browned—about 20 minutes. Serves 6.

There are times when deviled crab can be the most wonderful food on earth. They make a lovely brunch dish with a light champagne or a fine evening meal with a lightly chilled Alsatian Riesling.

Crab Collection

CAROL'S DEVILED CRABS NORFOLK

1 tablespoon melted butter
1 tablespoon flour
½ cup cream or milk
½ teaspoon seafood seasoning
salt and pepper to taste

Blend above ingredients together and let come to a boil, stirring constantly. Then add the following:

1 pound crab meat
2 hard-cooked eggs, chopped
½ teaspoon Worcestershire sauce

Blend well and place in crab shells. Brush with melted butter and cracker crumbs. Bake in slow oven at 275 degrees until well browned. Serves 4 to 6.

Try this classic recipe when you want to serve something special that doesn't take alot of time.

Carol Smith, Baltimore, Maryland

LEEDS CREEK DEVILED CRAB

½ small onion, finely chopped

2 large fresh mushrooms, finely chopped

1 clove garlic, finely chopped

4 tablespoons butter, 2 tablespoons melted

2 tablespoons flour

1½ teaspoons dry mustard

Tabasco sauce

⅛ teaspoon freshly grated nutmeg

1 teaspoon Worcestershire sauce

1 cup clam broth

2 egg yolks, beaten

1 pound crab meat

2 tablespoons cracker crumbs

Saute onion, mushrooms, and garlic in melted butter until soft. Stir in flour and seasonings, slowly add broth, stirring constantly. When sauce is smooth, remove from heat and stir in egg yolks carefully. Fold in crab meat. Pile into scallop shells. Sprinkle with cracker crumbs and dribble melted butter on tops. Bake at 400 degrees for 8 to 10 minutes until brown. Serves 6.

An interesting dish that's easy to do—try serving it with a crisp salad, crusty roll, and a little wine for an elegant dinner.

Crab Collection

DEVILED CRAB SOUFFLE

2 tablespoons butter
¼ cup flour
½ teaspoon salt
½ teaspoon powdered dry mustard
1 cup milk
3 egg yolks, beaten
2 tablespoons chopped fresh parsley
2 teaspoons grated onion
1 tablespoon lemon juice
1 pound crab meat
3 egg whites, beaten

Melt butter; blend in flour and seasonings. Add milk gradually and cook until thick and smooth, stirring constantly. Stir a little of the hot sauce into egg yolk; add to remaining sauce, stirring constantly. Add parsley, onion, lemon juice, and crab meat. Fold in egg white. Place in a well-greased 1 ½-quart casserole. Place casserole in a pan of hot water. Bake in a moderate oven, 350 degrees, for 1 hour or until souffle is firm in the center. Serve immediately. Serves 6.

Many of these recipes can be assembled in advance. Then, the dish can be popped into the oven as guests arrive. You can keep your eye on it and pull it out just when it's cooked to perfection.

Crab Collection

STUFFED CRAB WICOMICO

1 onion, chopped
1 green pepper, chopped
1 clove garlic, minced
½ cup melted butter
1 pound crab meat
1½ cups Italian bread crumbs, divided
¼ cup water
juice of 1 lemon
1 tablespoon chopped parsley
dash of Worcestershire sauce
dash of hot sauce
⅛ teaspoon cayenne pepper
salt and pepper to taste

Saute onion, green pepper, and garlic in butter 5 minutes. Add crab meat, ¾ cup bread crumbs, water, and lemon juice; simmer 20 minutes. Stir in parsley and remaining seasonings. Spoon into 12 crab shells. Combine butter and remaining bread crumbs, and sprinkle over crab mixture. Bake at 450 degrees for 3 to 5 minutes. Yields 12 servings.

Add your own creativity to this dish by varying a meat topping such as bacon or Smithfield ham. This flavorful dish would go well with a green vegetable and crisp salad.

Crab Collection

VIRGINIA DEVILED CRAB

2 tablespoons chopped onion
3 tablespoons butter, melted
2 tablespoons flour
¾ cup milk
½ teaspoon salt
dash pepper
½ teaspoon powdered mustard
1 teaspoon Worcestershire sauce
½ teaspoon sage
dash cayenne pepper
1 tablespoon lemon juice
1 egg, beaten
1 tablespoon chopped parsley
1 pound crab meat
1 tablespoon butter, melted
¼ cup dry bread crumbs

Cook onion in butter until tender. Blend in flour. Add milk gradually and cook until thick, stirring constantly. Add seasonings and lemon juice. Stir a little of the hot sauce into egg; add to remaining sauce, stirring constantly. Add parsley and crab meat. Place in six well-greased individual shells or 5-ounce custard cups. Combine butter and crumbs; sprinkle over top of each shell. Bake in a moderate oven, 350 degrees for 15 to 20 minutes or until brown. Serves 6.

Just thinking about the crab...

Virginia Institute of Marine Sciences, Gloucester Point, Virginia

DEVILED CRAB DELUXE

1 pound crab meat

1 cup cracker crumbs

1 tablespoon lemon juice

1 teaspoon Worcestershire sauce

½ cup minced onion

dash of hot sauce

dash of cayenne pepper

1 teaspoon dry mustard

¼ cup parsley flakes

⅔ cup butter, melted

¼ cup evaporated milk

salt and pepper as desired

½ cup cracker crumbs for topping

butter for topping

In bowl, mix first 12 ingredients lightly but thoroughly. Put mixture into six individual shells or ramekins. Sprinkle with cracker crumbs; dot with butter. Bake 15 to 20 minutes at 375 degrees or until browned on top. Yield 6 servings.

"Elegant and delicious" best describes this dish. Some good side dishes might be rice, a flavorful green vegetable, and a fruit salad.

Maryland Seafood Cookbook I

SPRING COVE DEVILED CRAB

½ cup butter

4 tablespoons onions, minced

½ cup flour

1½ teaspoons dry mustard

1½ teaspoons salt

4 cups whole milk

3 teaspoons Worcestershire sauce

6 teaspoons lemon juice

dash of hot pepper sauce

3 cups of celery, diced

2 tablespoons parsley, snipped

6 hard-cooked eggs, peeled and chopped

2 pounds crab meat

2 cups buttered bread crumbs

Combine butter, minced onions, flour, mustard, and salt in a saucepan and cook until frothy. Add milk and stir constantly until thick and smooth. Then add Worcestershire sauce, lemon juice, hot pepper sauce, celery, parsley, hard-cooked eggs, and crab meat. Spoon mixture into 16 oven-proof shells and top with bread crumbs. Bake at 400 degrees for 20 minutes. Yields 16 servings.

This dish has many complex flavors. I suggest an ale or even a dark beer as an accompaniment.

Crab Collection

CAMBRIDGE DEVILED CRAB

4 hard-cooked eggs
1 cup bread crumbs
1 pound crab meat
juice of 1 lemon
1 teaspoon Worcestershire sauce
2 tablespoons butter, melted
4 tablespoons mayonnaise
½ teaspoon salt
½ teaspoon pepper

Chop whites and yolks of eggs separately. Mix all other ingredients together in order listed then add eggs. Mix. Place in individual shells or baking dishes. Bake in 350-degree oven for 20 to 25 minutes. Serves 6.

Crab in almost any form is fit for a king, but rest assured that queens favored them, too.

Crab Collection

FALLSWOOD DEVILED CRAB

¾ cup milk

2 tablespoons onion, chopped

2 tablespoons celery, very finely minced

3 tablespoons butter

2 tablespoons flour

dash lemon juice

½ teaspoon dry mustard

1 teaspoon winter savory

1 teaspoon Worcestershire sauce

dash cayenne

salt and white pepper

1 egg, beaten

1 pound crab meat

2 tablespoons parsley, minced

buttered fine bread crumbs

Heat ½ cup of the milk while you saute the onion and celery in butter until they are translucent. Blend in flour and stir on low heat until flour has a chance to cook a little. The mixture will be a little foamy. Add hot milk and stir with a wire whisk. Add the lemon juice and all seasonings. Beat the egg in a bowl with ¼ cup milk. Stir in a little of the hot sauce to the egg and milk mixture; then add the mixture to the sauce in the pot. Add the crab meat and parsley. Reheat, stirring to blend well. Spoon into greased shells and top with buttered crumbs. Bake in a 350-degree oven for 15 to 20 minutes or until browned. Serves 6.

This recipe may be refrigerated or frozen before baking. When ready to serve, let it reach room temperature, then bake.

Crab Collection

DEALE DEVILED CRAB

½ cup chopped onion

⅓ cup chopped pepper

1 rib chopped celery

2 tablespoons butter

2 tablespoons flour

¾ cup milk

1 tablespoon lemon juice

1½ teaspoons dry mustard

1 teaspoon Worcestershire sauce

¼ teaspoon salt

¼ teaspoon black pepper

3 or 4 drops hot sauce

1 egg, beaten

1 tablespoon chopped parsley

1 pound crab meat

1 tablespoon melted butter

¼ cup dry bread crumbs

Saute onion, pepper, and celery in butter until transparent. Blend in flour. Add milk slowly to avoid lumping and cook until thick, stirring constantly. Add lemon juice and seasonings. Stir the hot sauce into the egg and add to sauce, stirring constantly. Add parsley and crab meat, blend well. Combine butter and crumbs; sprinkle over top of each 4-ounce ramekin or mock crab shell. Bake in preheated oven at 375 degrees for 20 to 25 minutes or until brown. Serves 6.

Another way to enjoy this recipe is to omit the last tablespoon of butter and add instead a ¼-inch strip of bacon and bake until done.

Crab Collection

MRS. GRAY'S DEVILED CRAB

1 pound crab meat

1 teaspoon to 1 tablespoon black pepper

¼ to ½ teaspoon red pepper

very little or no salt

1 tablespoon dry mustard, sifted between fingers so there are no lumps

½ stick butter, melted

1 egg, beaten

Pick meat, add seasonings, and mix. Add beaten egg and melted butter. Mix thoroughly. Pack in shells and broil 8 to 10 minutes until very brown. Taste before packing meat in shells. If it tastes fairly hot when cold, it's properly seasoned. It gets hotter as it cooks. Serves 6.

In my travels around the Chesapeake Bay, I always get requests for Mrs. Gray's recipe, so here it is. Now, give it a try.

Capital Newspaper, August 31, 1988

159

DEVILISH CRAB EGGS

1 cup crab meat

6 hard-cooked eggs

3 tablespoons finely chopped celery

4 heaping tablespoons mayonnaise

1 teaspoon dry mustard

¼ teaspoon salt

2 dashes pepper

¼ teaspoon parsley flakes

2 to 3 dashes oregano leaves

2 to 3 dashes garlic powder

4 drops Worcestershire sauce

Cut eggs in half lengthwise; remove yolks, put in bowl and mash well. Add celery, mayonnaise, and seasonings. Add crab meat and mix well. Stuff egg whites with yolk mixture. Chill before serving. Serves 6.

If Maryland is for crabs and Virginia is for lovers, then the Chesapeake Bay must be for crab lovers.

Crab Collection

BAYSIDE DEVILED CRAB

2 tablespoons chopped onion
2 tablespoons melted butter
2 tablespoons flour
¾ cup milk
1 tablespoon lemon juice
1½ teaspoons powdered mustard
1 teaspoon Worcestershire sauce
3 drops liquid hot pepper sauce
dash pepper
dash cayenne pepper
1 egg, beaten
1 tablespoon chopped parsley
1 pound crab meat
1 tablespoon melted butter
¼ cup dry bread crumbs, with chopped
   herbs added (thyme, dill, savory)

Cook onion in butter until tender. Blend in flour. Add milk gradually and cook until thick, stirring constantly. Add lemon juice and seasonings. Stir a little of the hot sauce into the egg; add to remaining sauce, stirring constantly. Add parsley and crab meat; blend well. Place in six well-greased individual shells or 5-ounce custard cups. Combine butter and crumbs; sprinkle over top of each shell. Bake in a moderate oven, 350 degrees for 20 to 25 minutes or until brown. Serves 6.

A few herbs in the crumb topping for this dish add a speedy and flavorful touch to the crab. Broccoli and a fruity salad would be nice meal accompaniments for this.

Crab Collection

POPES CREEK DEVILED CRAB

1 pound crab meat

2 hard-boiled eggs, finely chopped

3 tablespoons mayonnaise

2 tablespoons lemon juice

1 teaspoon Worcestershire sauce

1 teaspoon Dijon mustard

salt and red pepper (cayenne) to taste

¼ pound butter

1 tablespoon finely minced onion

1 to 2 cups freshly made bread crumbs

1 teaspoon baking powder

Combine crab meat with chopped eggs, mayonnaise, lemon juice, Worcestershire sauce, mustard, salt, and pepper. Mix gently and refrigerate for at least an hour. Meanwhile, melt butter, add onions, and saute until softened (but not browned), then stir in bread crumbs, setting aside ½ cup.

When ready to bake crabs, add the bread crumb mixture and baking powder to crab meat mixture and toss very lightly—with least possible mixing. Pile gently into crab shells; sprinkle with remaining bread crumbs and bake in moderate oven until golden brown. Serves 6.

Make your side dishes while this one bakes. Something like a marinated salad or a creamy cole slaw will round-out the texture and eye appeal of your meal.

Crab Collection

NORTHERN NECK STUFFED CRAB

1 pound crab meat
salt, pepper, capers, to taste
1 pimiento, diced
1 teaspoon melted butter
mayonnaise
1 whole garlic clove
olive oil
garlic dill pickles, for garnish

Mix crab meat with salt, pepper, and capers to taste. Add pimiento, melted butter, and enough mayonnaise to moisten. Rub six crab shells with garlic and olive oil. Heap mixture in shells, wrap shells in aluminum foil and heat over coals for about 20 to 25 minutes. Garnish with garlic dill pickles. Serves 6.

Surrounded by natural waterways and laced with creeks and inlets, the northern neck area of the Chesaspeake Bay is of natural and breathtaking beauty. It's no wonder the crabs harvested here are so tasty.

Crab Collection

DEVILED DUNGENESS CRAB CASSEROLE

½ cup finely chopped onion

¼ cup finely chopped green pepper

3 tablespoons butter

3 tablespoons flour

1½ cups half and half

2 egg yolks, beaten slightly

dash of cayenne

½ teaspoon salt

2 teaspoons Worcestershire sauce

1 tablespoon prepared mustard

1 tablespoon finely chopped chives

1¼ pounds crab meat

1 cup cracker crumbs

2 tablespoons melted butter

Heat oven to 375 degrees. Saute onion and green pepper in 3 tablespoons butter until tender in saucepan. Add flour; mix until smooth. Stir in half and half gradually; cook over medium heat, stirring constantly until sauce thickens. Stir a small amount of the hot sauce into egg yolks; add to remaining sauce in pan; heat 2 minutes. Remove from heat; add cayenne, salt, Worcestershire, mustard, and chives; mix well. Stir in crab meat. Spoon crab mixture in six buttered ramekins, custard cups, or 1-quart casserole. Combine crackers and 2 tablespoons melted butter; sprinkle on crab mixture. Bake for 20 to 25 minutes or until crumbs are golden brown. Serves 6.

The next time you entertain extra-special guests, dazzle them by serving this deviled casserole. Very few entrees match its elegance and eye appeal.

Crab Collection

Imperial Crab
and more...

CRAB IMPERIAL

1 pound backfin crab meat

2 tablespoons butter

2 tablespoons flour

¾ cup milk

1 egg, beaten

1 hard-cooked egg, chopped fine

1 tablespoon mayonnaise

6 drops Worcestershire sauce

½ teaspoon dry mustard

½ teaspoon parsley flakes

¼ teaspoon seafood seasoning

1 teaspoon salt

¼ teaspoon pepper

½ cup bread crumbs

¼ cup melted butter

pimiento for garnish

Put crab meat in large bowl. Melt butter over low heat. Add flour and stir to make paste. Add milk and cook slowly, stirring constantly, until thickened. Reserve 6 tablespoons white sauce; add remainder to crab meat, along with raw egg, hard-cooked egg, mayonnaise, Worcestershire sauce, mustard, parsley flakes, seafood seasoning, salt, and pepper. Mix gently but thoroughly. Put crab meat mixture into six baking shells or ramekins. Top each with bread crumbs, then melted butter, then reserved white sauce. Add pimiento strips for garnish. Bake at 350 degrees for 15 to 20 minutes or until browned on top. Yields 6 servings.

Crab imperial is just the dish for a warm summer's evening. Serve with a light appetizer and fruit kabobs to complete the meal with a splash of color.

Seafood Marketing Authority, Annapolis, Maryland

CAPE CHARLES CRAB IMPERIAL

1 green bell pepper, finely chopped
2 pimientos, finely chopped
2 tablespoons chives, finely chopped
1 tablespoon prepared English mustard
1 teaspoon salt
½ teaspoon white pepper
2 whole raw eggs
1 cup mayonnaise
3 pounds lump crab meat
mayonnaise
Old Bay Seasoning

Mix together first eight ingredients; add crab and toss very lightly. (Make certain lumps of crab are not broken, but the meat is covered with sauce.) Divide mixture into 12 shells or ramekins, heaping it lightly. Coat the top with a little mayonnaise; sprinkle with Old Bay Seasoning. Bake 15 minutes at 350 degrees. Serve hot or cold. Yields 12 servings.

The next time you entertain with crab imperial as your entree, you may want to set up a salad bar for your guests. Include one type of green for crispness, another for a soft, buttery quality, and a third for appearance.

Crab Collection

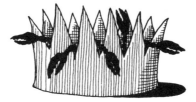

WARE RIVER IMPERIAL CRAB

1 pound lump crab meat

2 tablespoons capers

½ teaspoon dried mustard

1 teaspoon Worcestershire sauce

pinch of cayenne pepper

salt and pepper to taste

½ cup mayonnaise

butter

paprika to sprinkle

Mix first seven ingredients by tossing, avoid breaking crab meat lumps. Butter baking dish and place in dish. Put butter lump on top and sprinkle paprika on top. Bake in 375-degree oven for 20 to 30 minutes or until brown. Serves 6.

This dish is very easy to prepare, and it is a standard Bay recipe that has been around forever. Accompany it with lots of lager beer or a white table wine.

Crab Collection

COBB ISLAND CRAB IMPERIAL

1 pound crab meat (preferably backfin)
1 tablespoon butter
1 tablespoon flour
½ cup milk
1 teaspoon minced onion
1½ teaspoons Worcestershire sauce
2 slices white bread, cubed (crusts removed)
½ cup mayonnaise
1 tablespoon lemon juice
½ teaspoon salt
few dashes pepper
2 tablespoons butter
paprika, to sprinkle

In medium pan, melt butter, mix in flour. Slowly add milk, stirring constantly, to keep mixture smooth and free from lumps. Cook, stirring, over medium heat until mixture comes to a boil and thickens. Mix in onions, Worcestershire sauce, and bread cubes. Cool.

Fold in mayonnaise, lemon juice, salt and pepper.

In another pan, heat butter until lightly browned. Add crab meat and toss lightly. Combine with sauce mixture. Put mixture into individual shells or ramekins. Sprinkle paprika over top. Bake at 450 degrees until hot and bubbly and lightly browned on top, 10 to 15 minutes. Serves 4 to 6.

Crab imperial's special taste and lightness has made it a dinner favorite known round the world. Serve it with fruits or vegetables and your success will be guaranteed.

Crab Collection

CRAB IMPERIAL INDIAN CREEK

2 pounds crab meat
1 egg
⅔ cup finely diced green pepper
¼ cup finely diced pimiento
2 teaspoons dry mustard
2 teaspoons salt
¼ teaspoon white pepper
¾ cup mayonnaise
paprika

Beat egg in a medium-size bowl; stir in green pepper, pimiento, mustard, salt, pepper, and all but 2 tablespoons of the mayonnaise until well-blended. Fold in crab meat. Spoon into eight 10-ounce custard cups or individual baking dishes. Spread top of each with 1 teaspoon of the remaining mayonnaise; sprinkle with paprika. Bake in moderate oven (350 degrees) for 15 minutes or just until hot. Yields 8 servings.

This recipe has few ingredients but lots of flavor. Add watermelon, boiled corn, and a fresh tomato salad to compose a traditional menu.

Crab Collection

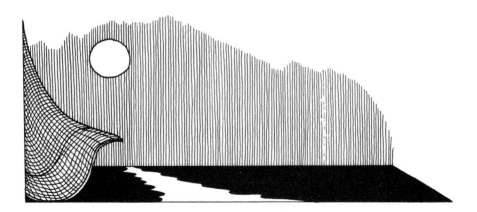

MILES RIVER CRAB IMPERIAL

1 green pepper, finely diced

2 pimientos, finely diced

1 tablespoon English mustard

1 teaspoon salt

½ teaspoon white pepper

2 whole eggs

1 cup mayonnaise

3 pounds lump crab meat

1 tablespoon mayonnaise

paprika to taste

Mix green pepper and pimientos, add mustard, salt, white pepper, eggs, and 1 cup mayonnaise. Mix well. Add crab meat and mix with fingers so the lumps are not broken. Divide mixture into 12 crab shells or casseroles, heaping it in lightly. Top with a thin coating of mayonnaise and sprinkle with a bit of paprika. Bake at 350 degrees for 15 minutes. Serve hot or cold. Serves 12.

'Tis the season to be crabby, and one of the delights of living around Maryland is the fresh crab meat available. We use this recipe frequently. You will, too.

Crab Collection

EASTPORT BAKED CRAB

1 pound crab meat

1⅓ cups chopped celery

1 cup mayonnaise

½ cup chopped onion

⅓ cup chopped green pepper

1 teaspoon Worcestershire sauce

½ teaspoon salt

½ cup soft bread crumbs

¼ cup grated sharp cheddar cheese

Combine crab meat, celery, mayonnaise, onion, green pepper, Worcestershire sauce, and salt. Place crab meat mixture into a well-greased 2-quart casserole. Combine bread crumbs and cheese; sprinkle over top of crab mixture. Bake in moderate oven at 350 degrees for 25 to 30 minutes or until thoroughly heated and crumbs are lightly browned. Serves 6.

I love the simple elegance of this dish which looks as lovely as it is good to eat. Try it with a lightly chilled Sauterne wine. It has just the amount of flavor to balance the meal.

Crab Collection

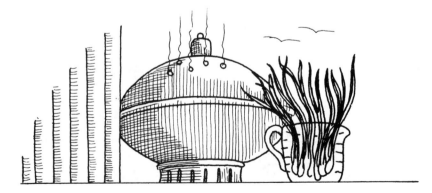

CRAB MIDDLETON

½ cup chopped celery
½ cup chopped mushrooms
¼ pound butter
1 cup mayonnaise
1 tablespoon dry mustard
1½ tablespoons Old Bay seasoning
1 pound backfin crab meat
buttered bread crumbs

In large skillet, saute celery and mushrooms in butter until tender. Cool and mix with mayonnaise. Add mustard, seasoning, and crab meat. Put in casserole dish and top with buttered bread crumbs. Bake 20 minutes at 350 degrees. Serves 6.

Whether you are a gourmet or gourmand, connoisseur or casual cook, you will enjoy preparing this tasty recipe.

Middleton Tavern, Annapolis, Maryland

CRABTOWN CRAB

¾ cup butter
½ teaspoon salt
pinch black pepper
pinch cayenne pepper
pinch garlic powder
1½ teaspoons lemon juice
¼ cup dry sherry
1 pound crab meat
paprika for garnish

Melt butter in pan. Add seasonings, lemon juice, and sherry. Remove from heat and gently mix in crab meat.

Put mixture in six individual ramekins or in 1-quart shallow baking dish. Sprinkle paprika over top. Bake at 350 degrees until piping hot, about 10 to 15 minutes. Serve at once. Yields 6 servings.

Some dishes are timeless. This is one of them. Try it for lunch with a light Chardonnay or a Chesapeake blanc. Fill out the meal with fresh baked bread and a tossed green salad.

Seafood Marketing Authority, Annapolis, Maryland

TAPPAHANNOCK CRAB CASSEROLE

3 tablespoons butter
3 tablespoons flour
1 teaspoon salt
⅛ teaspoon black pepper
⅛ teaspoon mustard
1½ cups milk
½ teaspoon Worcestershire sauce
dash hot sauce
¼ cup grated Parmesan cheese
1 pound crab meat
1 (1-pound) can artichoke hearts, drained
½ cup buttered bread crumbs
¼ cup grated Parmesan cheese

Melt butter; stir in flour, salt, pepper, and mustard until smooth. Gradually add milk and cook until thickened, stirring constantly. Add Worcestershire sauce, hot sauce, ¼ cup Parmesan cheese, and crab meat; mix well.

Arrange artichoke hearts in bottom of a 1 ½-quart casserole. Spoon in crab mixture. Top with buttered bread crumbs which have been mixed with ¼ cup Parmesan cheese. Bake at 350 degrees for 30 to 40 minutes. Serves 6 to 8.

We found this recipe to be especially good and an easy meal for all occasions. Drink a well-chilled, first-rate Chardonnay with this dish.

Crab Collection

175

MOBJACK IMPERIAL CRAB

½ cup milk
1½ teaspoons butter
1 tablespoon flour
1 egg yolk, well beaten
½ teaspoon dry mustard
½ teaspoon cayenne pepper
¼ teaspoon celery salt
¼ teaspoon salt
¼ teaspoon pepper
1½ teaspoons lemon juice
½ teaspoon Worcestershire sauce
2 tablespoons mayonnaise
1 pound backfin crab meat
1 tablespoon milk
parsley

Heat ½ cup milk to the boiling point. Melt the butter, add flour, pour heated milk over the butter and flour, beat until creamy, and allow to cool. Add egg, seasonings, lemon juice, and 1 tablespoon of mayonnaise, blending well. Add crab and toss lightly. Fill crab shells or small dishes. Mix remaining mayonnaise with 1 tablespoon of milk and brush on top. Finally, sprinkle with parsley. Bake at 400 degrees for 8 to 10 minutes or until brown. Serves 4 to 6.

Great for a brunch or lunch—this crab imperial has a company-good flavor. Serve it with fruit or a green vegetable.

Crab Collection

CRAB SNUG HARBOR

1 cup sliced celery
¼ cup butter
1 cup sliced fresh mushrooms
¼ cup sliced green onions
3 tablespoons flour
¾ teaspoon salt
dash white pepper
1 cup milk
½ cup half-and-half
¼ cup sherry
½ teaspoon Worcestersshire sauce
1 pound crab meat
2 tablespoons diced pimiento
6 servings hot, fluffy rice
1 ripe avocado, peeled and sliced

Cook celery in butter until tender. Add mushrooms and onion, and cook until onion is tender. Blend in flour, salt, and pepper. Stir in milk and half-and-half; cook until thickened, stirring constantly. Add sherry, Worcestershire sauce, crab meat, and pimiento; mix carefully. Place over low heat and bring to serving temperature, stirring often. Serve on rice; garnish with avocado slices. Serves 6.

Almost everyone on the Chesapeake Bay has a favorite crab imperial recipe. The addition of hot, fluffy rice creates yet another elegant dish.

Crab Collection

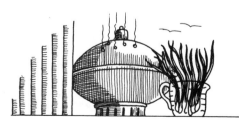

ANGIE'S CRAB IMPERIAL

2 tablespoons butter
½ onion, chopped
2 tablespoons green pepper, chopped
1 pound lump crab meat
½ teaspoon salt
dash cayenne pepper
1 teaspoon garlic powder
1 teaspoon mustard
dash Worcestershire sauce
2 egg yolks
2 cups heavy cream
bread crumbs and butter

Heat butter and saute onion; add crab meat, green pepper, seasonings, and cream; and mix well. Bind with egg yolks and pile into shells or ramekins. Sprinkle with crumbs, dot with butter, and bake at 350 degrees for 15 to 20 minutes or until brown. Serves 4 to 6.

Everyone raves about Angie's Crab Imperial. This delicious imperial was created on the shores of the Anacostia River.

Angie Machetto, Washington, D.C.

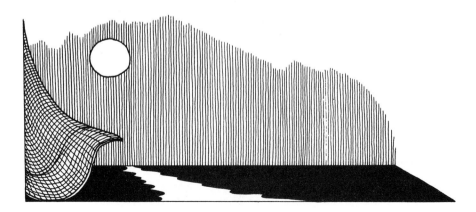

CRAB MEAT NORFOLK

2 tablespoons butter
juice of half lemon
1 pound crab meat
salt and pepper to taste
paprika
2 tablespoons minced parsley
4 slices buttered toast

Heat the butter and juice of half a lemon in skillet. Add the crab meat, salt, and pepper. Shake skillet to mingle flavors. When mixture is hot, dust with paprika and garnish with parsley. Serve on slices of buttered toast. Serves 4.

Tidewater Virginia is home to this delicious recipe, and every restaurant has its own version. Give it a try. I think you will be delighted with the results.

"The Official Crab Eater's Guide"

CRAB AND VEGETABLE CASSEROLE

¼ cup olive oil

½ large onion, sliced thin

2 stalks celery, sliced

3 medium zucchini or green squash, sliced thin

3 tablespoons chopped garlic

½ pound cleaned spinach

1 10-ounce can whole peeled tomatoes, crushed lightly (or 3 garden ripe tomatoes, diced large)

3 pounds crab meat

½ cup dry white wine

large pinch chopped parsley

pinch thyme

pinch basil

fresh ground black pepper

2 ounces fresh grated Parmesan cheese

rice

In a large skillet or saute pan, heat oil. Saute onion, celery, and zucchini until tender. Add garlic, spinach, and tomatoes and heat through. Add crab meat and wine and season with parsley, thyme, basil, and black pepper. Pour into large casserole and top with grated Parmesan cheese. Finish in hot oven until heated through. Serve with rice. Serves 12.

Chef Bil's use of fresh-picked herbs is the key in this recipe. It is a real plus, and one that we're sure you will enjoy.

Bil Shockley, Neptune's Seafood Pub, North Beach, Maryland

OXFORD CRAB CASSEROLE

1 cup sour cream
⅓ cup grated Parmesan cheese
1 tablespoon lemon juice
1 tablespoon grated onion
½ teaspoon salt
dash Tabasco sauce
2 pounds crab meat
¾ cup soft bread cubes
1 tablespoon melted butter
paprika

Combine sour cream, cheese, lemon juice, onion, salt, and Tabasco; mix thoroughly. Pour over crab meat and mix lightly. Place in six well-greased individual shells or custard cups. Combine bread cubes and butter; sprinkle over top of crab mixture. Sprinkle with paprika. Bake in a moderate oven, 350 degrees, for 25 to 30 minutes or until lightly browned. Serves 6.

Serve with a Beaujolais wine—its light and fruity flavor does not overpower the crab, yet it stands up to the pungency of the Parmesan cheese and lemon.

Crab Collection

COLONIAL BEACH CRACKER CRAB

1 tablespoon butter
medium onion, chopped fine
2 tablespoons green pepper, chopped
2 tablespoons chopped celery
dash salt and pepper
1 teaspoon mustard
1 tablespoon lemon juice
1 pound crab meat
¼ cup cracker crumbs
4 ounces cream
½ cup grated sharp cheese

Place butter into frying pan and saute onion, green pepper, and celery. Add salt and pepper, mustard, lemon juice, crab meat, and cracker crumbs. Steam together for 2 to 3 minutes. Add cream and mix well. Pour into a greased flat pyrex baking dish. Bake about 45 minutes at 350 degrees. During the last several minutes of baking time, add the sharp cheese and bake until melted and a little brown. Serves 6.

This hot cracker crab brings back many memories of summer at the beach. What great fun we had, and what good food we enjoyed. I can't wait to return.

Louise Tierney, Waldorf, Maryland

182

BAKED CRAB MEAT REMICK

1 pound crab meat

6 strips crisp bacon

1 teaspoon dry mustard

½ teaspoon paprika

1 teaspoon celery salt

few drops Tabasco sauce

½ cup chili sauce

1 teaspoon tarragon vinegar

1¾ cups mayonnaise

Pile crab meat in six baking casseroles. Heat in oven and top each with strip of bacon. Blend mustard, paprika, celery salt, and Tabasco. Add chili sauce and vinegar; mix well. Add mayonnaise. Spread the hot crab meat with this sauce and glaze under broiler flame. Yields 6 servings.

This recipe was adapted from one that was printed in Southern Living Cookbook circa 1970. The last few times I prepared this dish, I substituted Old Bay Seafood Seasoning for the paprika and I cut back the mayonnaise to 1 cup. It was delicious.

Sue and Bob Chapman, Nokesville, Virginia

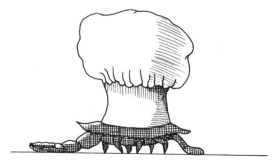

CRAB ROMANOFF

2 cups hot cooked rice

1 8-ounce container sour cream

1 8-ounce container cottage cheese

2 tablespoons finely chopped green pepper

2 tablespoons chopped chives

1 tablespoon Worcestershire sauce

½ teaspoon salt

⅛ teaspoon cayenne pepper

2 to 3 dashes garlic powder

1 4-ounce can mushrooms, drained

1 pound Maryland crab meat

2 tablespoons grated American cheese

paprika, for garnish

In a large bowl, mix rice, sour cream, cottage cheese, green pepper, and seasonings. Add mushrooms and crab meat; mix gently but thoroughly. Put mixture into greased 2-quart casserole. Sprinkle cheese, then paprika, over top. Bake at 350 degrees until hot and bubbly, about 20 minutes. Serves 6.

You can enjoy more of Maryland by ordering the "Maryland Seafood Cookbook." Choose from three colorful editions, each illustrating different ways to enjoy the bounties of the Chesapeake Bay. Write to: P.O. Box 1589, Annapolis, Maryland 21404.

Developed by Seafood Marketing Authority, Annapolis, Maryland

CRAB MEAT ROYALE

½ cup chopped mushrooms or 1 4-ounce
   can, drained
½ stick butter
1 tablespoon chopped onion
1 pound crab meat
1 teaspoon Worcestershire sauce
¼ cup dry sherry
3 tablespoons flour
1 cup milk
salt and pepper to taste
grated cheese for topping

In large fry pan, saute mushrooms in butter for 5 minutes. Add onion and cook until onion is tender. Add crab meat, Worcestershire sauce and sherry.

Make a paste of the flour and milk. Add to crab meat mixture and cook until sauce thickens. Add salt and pepper.

Put mixture into baking dish or individual shells or ramekins. Sprinkle grated cheese over top. Bake at 350 degrees for 5 minutes, or until cheese melts and mixture is bubbly. Makes 6 servings, about ½ cup each.

This is a great dish for guests. Add sweet potatoes, a green vegetable, and a garden salad to prepare a colorful and tasty meal.

Developed by Seafood Marketing Authority, Annapolis, Maryland

COOKIE'S CRAB IMPERIAL

4 tablespoons chopped green pepper

2 tablespoons chopped onion

4 tablespoons mayonnaise

1 pound backfin crab meat

2 tablespoons butter

2 tablespoons pimiento

2 eggs, beaten

2 teaspoons dry mustard

½ pound steamed shelled shrimp

Heat butter. Add green pepper, onion, and pimiento. Saute until tender. Combine eggs, dry mustard, mayonnaise, and crab meat. Add sauteed vegetables and mix. Layer the bottom of baking dish with shrimp. Spoon crab mixture over the shrimp and bake at 350 degrees for about 15 minutes or until a very light brown on top. Serves 6.

Crab and shrimp combine their wonderful flavors to make this wonderful entree.

Cookie Benner, New Carrolton, Maryland

RAPPAHANNOCK CRAB STUFFING

1 pound crab meat

½ cup chopped onion

⅓ cup chopped celery

⅓ cup chopped green pepper

2 cloves garlic, minced

⅓ cup melted butter

2 cups soft bread crumbs

3 eggs, beaten

1 tablespoon chopped parsley

1 teaspoon salt

½ teaspoon pepper

Cook onion, celery, green pepper, and garlic in butter until tender, but not brown. Combine all ingredients and mix well. Makes enough stuffing for six flounder, ¾ pound each, or one 4-pound flounder. Serves 6.

For variations in this recipe, the basic stuffing can be augmented to make crab cakes or deviled crab.

Crab Collection

CATLINS CRAB MEAT CASSEROLE

1 pound blue crab meat

2 tablespoons chopped onion

2 tablespoons melted fat or oil

2 tablespoons flour

¾ cup milk

1 tablespoon lemon juice

1½ teaspoon powdered mustard

1 teaspoon Worcestershire sauce

½ teaspoon salt

3 drops Tabasco

dash pepper

dash cayenne pepper

1 egg, beaten

1 tablespoon chopped parsley

1 tablespoon melted fat or oil

¼ cup dry bread crumbs

Cook onion in fat until tender. Blend in flour. Add milk gradually and cook until thick, stirring constantly. Add lemon juice and seasonings. Stir a little of the hot sauce into the egg; add to remaining sauce, stirring constantly. Add parsley and crab meat; blend well.

Place in six well-greased, individual shells or 5-ounce custard cups. Combine fat and crumbs; sprinkle over top of each shell. Bake in a moderate oven, 350 degrees, for 20 to 25 minutes or until brown. Serves 6.

This recipe was one of several that were featured in a newspaper story about Maryland crab fanciers.

Mrs. John Catlins, Crisfield, Maryland

CORRINE'S CRAB MEAT CASSEROLE

1 pound crab meat
1 small can peas
1 can condensed mushroom soup
¼ teaspoon white pepper
½ cup grated cheese
dash hot sauce
1 tablespoon pimiento, cut in small pieces
1 tablespoon dry mustard
¼ teaspoon celery salt
paprika

Mix all ingredients and place into greased casserole dish, top with paprika. Bake in oven at 350 degrees for 20 minutes. Serves 4 to 6.

The "Galley Kiss Cookbook" was written for people on the go. Corrine's quick and easy recipe is one you will prepare again and again, so that you can go, go, go.

Corrine Kanter, Marathon Keys, Florida

DEEP-DISH CRAB PIE

½ cup finely chopped carrot

2 tablespoons butter

¼ cup ½-inch slices green onions

1 teaspoon dill weed

1 teaspoon basil

1 pound crab meat

1 unbaked pie shell in 10-inch quiche pan

1 can (13 ounces) evaporated milk

5 eggs

3 tablespoons dry sherry

1 tablespoon prepared mustard

½ teaspoon salt

In medium-size skillet, cook carrot in butter until tender. Add onions, dill weed, and basil; cook 1 minute. Remove from heat; stir in crab meat. Spoon into shell. Beat remaining ingredients. Pour over crab mixture. Bake on bottom rack of preheated 325-degree oven 50 to 55 minutes until knife inserted near center comes out clean. Let stand 15 minutes. Serves 6.

I clipped this from the "Shortcut Cook." It was a discussion on how to get more mileage out of a convenience food by using evaporated milk. The results are delicious.

Woman's Day Magazine, September 1, 1984

IMPOSSIBLE CRAB MEAT PIE

½ pound crab meat

4-ounce jar sliced mushrooms, drained

2 cups shredded Monterey Jack cheese

4 eggs

1 cup dairy sour cream

1 cup small curd creamed cottage cheese

½ cup prepared baking mix, such as Bisquick

⅛ teaspoon cayenne pepper

Heat oven to 350 degrees. Grease 10-inch pie plate. Layer crab meat, mushrooms, and Monterey Jack cheese in plate. Place remaining ingredients in blender container. Cover and blend on high about 1½ minutes until smooth (or beat 2-3 minutes on high speed of electric mixer, scraping bowl occasionally). Pour into plate. Bake about 45 minutes, until knife inserted in center comes out clean. Cool 5 minutes. Serves 6.

When relatives and friends descend for visits, there's nothing better to serve than a delicious crab pie.

The Capital Newspaper, Annapolis, Maryland

HORN POINT CRAB PIE

1 pastry shell
½ pound crab meat
1 cup Swiss cheese
½ cup chopped onions
4 eggs
2 cups half-and-half
¾ teaspoon salt
¼ teaspoon pepper
1 teaspoon red pepper

Combine crab meat, cheese, onions, and spices. Beat eggs. Add half-and-half and blend all ingredients. Pour into pastry shell. Bake at 425 degrees for 15 minutes. Reduce heat to 300 degrees and continue baking for 30 minutes or until knife inserted comes out clean. Serves 6.

Add a green salad to create a holiday atmosphere with this easy buffet lunch. Cut pie into slender wedges to give everyone a taste. Serve with fresh fruit.

Crab Collection

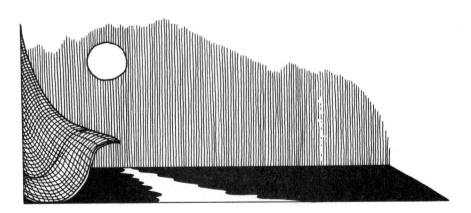

BACK CREEK CRAB PIE

1 8-ounce package soft cream cheese
1 teaspoon chopped onion
¾ teaspoon Old Bay Seafood Seasoning
½ cup chili sauce
½ cup catsup
1 tablespoon horseradish
1 teaspoon lemon juice
1 pound crab meat
crackers

Combine cream cheese, chopped onion, and Old Bay; spread on platter. Refrigerate covered with plastic wrap. Then make sauce by mixing remaining ingredients except crab meat and crackers. Spread over cheese. Just before serving, cover cheese and sauce with crab meat. Serve with crackers. Serves 6 to 8.

The use of freshly picked crab meat is a must in this recipe. Just watch it go!

Crab Collection

CRAB-STUFFED RED SNAPPER

⅓ cup minced onion

3 tablespoons butter

½ pound crab meat

½ cup fresh bread crumbs

¼ cup fresh chopped parsley

¼ cup heavy cream

1 teaspoon lemon thyme

4-pound red snapper, dressed for stuffing

salt and pepper

⅓ cup dry white wine mixed with ⅓ cup
    melted butter

    Saute onion in butter until golden. Remove from heat and mix in the crab meat, bread crumbs, parsley, heavy cream and lemon thyme. Sprinkle cavity of fish lightly with salt and pepper. Stuff the fish and skewer edges securely. Place fish in a greased baking pan, pour wine-butter mixture over fish. Bake in 400-degree oven, uncovered for 30 minutes or just until the flesh is opaque, basting frequently with wine sauce. Serves 4 to 6.

If you feel in the mood to experiment, many different kinds of fish can be found at your local seafood market. There are fascinating discoveries ahead for people with some imagination and initiative.

Crab Collection

IMPERIAL CRAB NORTH BEACH

1 pound claw crab meat
1 pound rockfish fillet
1 pint water
3 tablespoons chopped onion
1 tablespoon lemon juice
4 tablespoons butter
4 tablespoons flour
½ cup bread crumbs
½ cup milk
½ cup rockfish broth
¾ teaspoon salt
½ teaspoon Worcestershire sauce
dash of Tabasco sauce

Boil rockfish in 1 pint of water with ¼ teaspoon salt until it will flake. Pour off broth and save ½ cup. Cook onion in butter until tender, and blend in flour. Add ½ cup milk and ½ cup rockfish broth and cook until thick, stirring constantly. Flake the cooked rockfish fillet, and remove any shell from crab meat. Carefully tumble them together with ½ cup bread crumbs. Add seasonings, fish flakes, and crab meat to sauce and carefully mix. Place in about 12 greased crab shells, artificial shells, or custard cups. Bake at about 350 degrees for 20 to 25 minutes or until slightly brown. Yields 12 servings.

The next time you entertain extra-special guests, dazzle them by serving rockfish and crab meat. Very few entrees match its elegance and eye appeal.

Crab Collection

MARINATED CRAB CLAWS

3 quarts water
⅓ cup salt
crab boil
3 pounds fresh crab claws
1 cup minced green onion
½ cup minced parsley
2 stalks celery, minced
3 cloves garlic, crushed
1 cup olive oil
½ cup tarragon vinegar
2 tablespoons lemon juice

Combine water and salt in a Dutch oven; add crab boil according to package directions. Bring water to a boil; add crab claws. Cover and return to boiling point. Reduce heat and simmer 5 to 8 minutes or until crab claws are bright red.

Drain; let cool long enough to handle. Remove shell from large portion of crab claw. Place crab claws in a large shallow baking dish.

Combine remaining ingredients in a jar; shake well. Pour marinade over crab claws. Cover tightly and chill 4 to 5 hours.

Remove crab claws and reserve marinade. Yield: 5 to 6 servings.

Serve Marinated Crab Claws with French bread, and use the marinade as a dipping sauce.

Crab Collection

SIZZLING DUNGENESS CRAB LEGS

1½ pounds Dungeness crab legs, cooked
and shelled

⅓ cup melted, unsalted butter

⅓ cup lemon juice

1 garlic clove, minced

paprika

Marinate the crab legs for 2 hours in butter with lemon juice and minced garlic clove. Garnish with paprika. Broil til hot and sizzling. Serves 4 as a main course.

Deceptively simple and surprisingly unique in flavor, this Dungeness delight is so rich—so good.

Crab Collection

CRAB MEAT ALFREDO

4 pounds lump crab meat

2 cloves fresh garlic, finely chopped

4 red peppers, cut julienne

2 ounces clarified butter

1 quart heavy cream

2½ pounds egg-cheese tortellini

2½ pounds spinach-cheese tortellini

3 to 4 ounces Parmesan cheese

1 bunch scallions, chopped

salt and pepper to taste

Saute crab meat, garlic, and peppers in butter for 30 to 45 seconds. Add heavy cream, allow to heat through. Once cream is hot, add tortellinis and allow to heat through. Sprinkle Parmesan cheese over top and stir in gently. Let cream and cheese blend to thicken. Sprinkle in scallions for color and flavor with salt and pepper. Serves about 40 5-ounce portions.

This recipe may be served as an entree or an appetizer.

Longfellow's Restaurant, St. Michaels, Maryland

SOUTH MOUNTAIN MUSHROOM CAPS

1 large onion, chopped
2 pounds large mushrooms
1 teaspoon basil
1 tablespoon parsley
1 green pepper, chopped
1 teaspoon dry mustard
bread crumbs
½ pound Monterey Jack cheese
1 pound crab meat
butter

Saute mushroom stems in butter with basil, onion, parsley, pepper, dry mustard, and bread crumbs. Cool. Add in crab meat. Stuff mixture in mushroom caps, top with grated cheese, and bake at 350 degrees for about 20 minutes or until stuffing mixture is golden brown. Serves 4 to 6.

This mushroom dish is easy to prepare in little time, and there is virtually no clean up. Guests love it.

South County Dukes, Keedysville, Maryland

GULF COAST CRAB CREOLE

1 large onion, chopped
1 clove garlic, crushed
½ cup green pepper, chopped
4 tablespoons bacon fat
1 pound crab meat
16-ounce can tomatoes
½ cup celery, chopped
1 teaspoon sugar
1 teaspoon Worcestershire sauce
dash hot pepper sauce
½ teaspoon salt
⅛ teaspoon pepper
cooked rice

In a large skillet, saute onions, garlic, and green pepper in bacon fat until tender. Add remaining ingredients and simmer for 20 minutes. Serve over rice. Serves 4.

Along the rural byways of the south, sophisticated cuisine has evolved into classic dishes such as crab creole. The result is delicious.

Crab Collection

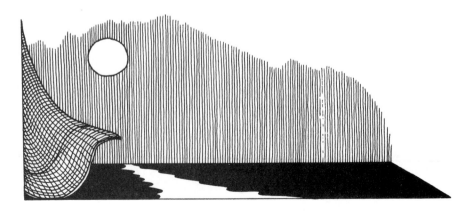

CRAB MEAT CARMODY

1 pound crab meat
2 cloves garlic, chopped
¼ pound butter
½ bunch shallots, chopped
1 green pepper, chopped
1 tablespoon flour
1 cup milk
6 sprigs parsley, chopped
½ cup sherry
1 cup bread crumbs
12 anchovy strips
4 tablespoons Fortina cheese, grated

Prepare crab meat. Saute garlic in butter until half brown. Add shallots and green pepper. Cook slowly until done, but not brown. Add flour and stir in well. Add milk and parsley; stir until thick. Add sherry. Fold in crab meat. Sprinkle in bread crumbs. Mold into balls and place on round, crisp toast. Lay two strips of anchovies on top of each. Sprinkle with Fortina cheese. Place under broiler until brown. Serves 6.

This recipe is tasty anytime of the year. Be sure to plan ahead and prepare a green salad to serve on the side.

Crab Collection

STONEY CREEK CRAB MEAT DIVAN

1 bunch broccoli, steamed and coarsely
    chopped
1 pound crab meat
1 cup mornay sauce (see below)
¼ cup seasoned bread crumbs

Cover the bottom of a shallow baking dish with chopped broccoli. Top with crab meat. Cover with mornay sauce and sprinkle with bread crumbs for baking to a golden brown. Bake 25 minutes at 350 degrees. Serves 6.

MORNAY SAUCE

2 tablespoons butter
1 cup milk or cream
¼ cup each grated Parmesan and Swiss
    cheese
2 tablespoons flour
salt and pepper to taste

Melt butter. Add flour and blend well. Slowly add milk, stirring constantly. As mixture thickens, add grated cheeses. Season to taste with salt and pepper.

Crab meat divan makes an impressive display in an informal setting. Enjoy!

Crab Collection

ANNIE'S STEWED HARD CRABS

1 dozen live hard crabs

water

3 strips of bacon

1 medium onion, chopped

6 small potatoes, diced

salt and pepper

flour to thicken

Completely clean hard crabs down to just the body and cut in half. Add water to cover crabs in cook pot. Add bacon. Cover and simmer for 30 minutes. Add onion, potatoes, salt, and pepper and cook until potatoes are tender. Stir in thickening made with flour and water. Stir until thickened. Serves 4.

Crisfield's first lady crabber, Crabbin' Annie, as she was better known, "could toss a double crab in the air and seperate the Jimmy from the female as she caught them in mid-air." (Quote from the Crisfield Times.)

Annie White Parkinson Nelson

GABE'S CRAB SUPREME

4 tablespoons butter
2 tablespoons flour
1½ cups condensed milk
½ teaspoon dry mustard
3 tablespoons grated Parmesan cheese
salt
1 egg yolk, lightly beaten
1 pound crab meat
12 shrimp, steamed and shelled
1 can button mushrooms, drained
2 tablespoons sherry

Make a cream sauce of 2 tablespoons butter, flour, and condensed milk; blend in mustard and 2 tablespoons cheese. Simmer a moment and salt to taste. Mix a little of the sauce with egg yolk; stir quickly into sauce. Add 1 tablespoon butter and combine with crab meat, shrimp, and mushrooms. Add sherry. Pour into 1½-quart casserole. Sprinkle with cheese and dot with remaining butter. Bake in 400-degree oven 15 minutes or until well heated and brown on top. Serves 6.

This crab dish is as appealing on the table as it is to the taste.

Gabe Fleri, Chevy Chase, Maryland

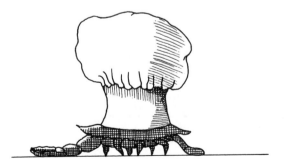

NEPTUNES NOODLES WITH CRAB MEAT SAUCE

5 ounces fine egg noodles
salted water
2 tablespoons oil
1 onion, chopped
½ cup Chinese cabbage
1 pound crab meat
1 cup chicken stock
salt
1 teaspoon corn starch
¼ cup cold water
½ cup watercress
1 teaspoon soy sauce

Boil noodles in salted water 5 minutes. Drain and keep warm. Heat oil, brown onion, and add Chinese cabbage. Add crab meat, chicken stock, seasoning, and simmer 5 minutes. Add cornstarch dissolved in cold water. Stir until thickened. Add chopped watercress and soy sauce and serve over hot noodles. Serves 6.

The God of the Sea, King Neptune, would surely approve of the simple and pure flavor of this dish. On one of those warm, early spring evenings, serve it with a dry chablis and an herbed cherry tomato salad for an impeccable seafood supper.

Crab Collection

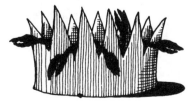

CRAB AND COUNTRY HAM

6 to 8 very thin slices of country ham
1 pound backfin crab meat
salt and pepper
cayenne
½ teaspoon dry mustard
½ teaspoon thyme
1 or 2 lemons
melted butter, about ¼ cup

Grease with butter a shallow, oven-proof dish (an oval shape is best). Line dish with cold, cooked slices of country ham, making sure both bottom and sides are covered. Mix crab meat in a bowl with spices—salt and pepper to taste, cayenne, dry mustard, and thyme. Spread crab meat over ham slices, being careful not to break up the lumps. Sprinkle all over with juice squeezed from lemons and then pour melted butter over all. Place under broiler until crab is slightly brown and bubbly and ham is warmed through. Serve immediately, making sure each person receives some of the ham. Serves 6-8.

This bountiful dish will delight and satisfy eight people. It's perfect for an easy lunch or a late night treat. Crab and ham are traditional fare served all over the south.

Crab Collection

206

ZIPPY CRAB IMPERIAL

2 tablespoons butter
1 cup green and red bell peppers, chopped
1 cup light cream
1 teaspoon vinegar
1 tablespoon Worcestershire sauce
½ teaspoon dry mustard
1 teaspoon salt
¼ teaspoon cayenne pepper
1 pound crab meat
1 cup bread crumbs

Melt butter in pan and saute peppers until soft. Add cream and seasonings and cook until thickened. Gently mix in the crab meat and bread crumbs. Transfer to a buttered casserole dish and bake at 325 degrees 10 to 15 minutes or until heated through. Serves 6.

Close your eyes and, if your taste buds have such a memory, think of the sweet, tender butter-drenched meat of the blue crab.

Crab Collection

CRAB CORN PUDDING

4 cups milk

1 cup yellow corn meal

2 tablespoons sugar

¼ teaspoon salt

pinch cayenne pepper

4 eggs

½ cup unsalted butter, melted and cooled

1¼ teaspoons baking powder

1 pound crab meat

2 cups fresh corn kernels

In a large deep saucepan, bring the milk to a boil over medium-high heat. Stir in the yellow corn meal, sugar, salt, and cayenne pepper. Let the mixture return to a boil, then reduce heat to a simmer. Stir often and continue to simmer for 5 to 6 minutes. Remove from heat and let cool for 10 minutes.

In a large bowl, whisk together the eggs, melted butter and baking powder. Stir in the corn kernels. Add the milk-corn meal mixture and stir to combine. Gently fold in crab to avoid breaking up lumps.

Pour the mixture into a well-buttered 2½-quart souffle dish, casserole, or any other straight-sided baking dish. Bake on the center rack of a preheated 350-degree oven for 45 minutes to 1 hour, or until the pudding is lightly puffed, lightly browned, and a knife or straw inserted in the center comes out clean. Serve immediately. Serves 12.

The American Indians first introduced popping corn to the Colonists by heaping it over burning embers. I wonder who tossed the crab on the fire.

USA Weekend Magazine, November 1987

SOUTHSIDE CRAB SOUFFLE

3 tablespoons butter
¼ cup flour
1½ teaspoons salt
½ teaspoon powdered mustard
1 cup milk
3 egg yolks, beaten
2 tablespoons chopped parsley
2 teaspoons grated onion
1 tablespoon lemon juice
1 pound crab meat
3 egg whites, beaten

Melt butter; blend in flour and seasonings. Add milk gradually and cook until thick and smooth, stirring constantly. Stir a little of the hot sauce into egg yolks, add to remaining sauce, stirring constantly. Add parsley, onion, lemon juice, and crab meat. Fold in egg whites. Place in a well-greased 1½-quart casserole. Place casserole in a pan of hot water. Bake in a moderate oven at 350 degrees for 1 hour or until souffle is firm in the center. Serve immediately. Serves 6.

There is something almost playful about the combination of ingredients in this souffle. The result is a bright and smiling luncheon treat.

Crab Collection

STIR-FRIED CRABS CANTONESE STYLE

8 live blue crabs

3 tablespoons liquid oil

2 to 3 cloves garlic, chopped

6 to 8 spring onions, chopped

1 tablespoon fresh ginger root, chopped

1 tablespoon fermented salted black beans, mashed

1 cup chicken stock

1 to 500 red peppers (depending on how hot you like your food)

Kill the crabs with an ice pick or by dropping in boiling water. Remove the legs, top shell, internal organs, and discard. Break the remaining body in half (it is traditional to leave the backfin attached). Heat a wok or skillet to high heat and add the oil. Stir fry the crab body halves and claws for 4 to 5 minutes until claws are bright red. Add garlic, onions, ginger root, red peppers, and black beans; stir fry another 1 to 2 minutes. Add chicken stock and reduce heat. Cover and cook for about 10 minutes. Uncover and increase heat to reduce sauce. Stir frequently until done. Serves 2 to 4.

The black beans are an essential ingredient; they give the dish its unique flavor. These beans are sold in small bottles in Chinese markets and last indefinitely without refrigeration. They are very strong in flavor, so be careful not to add too many. Mash them with a spoon before adding to the dish.

Jack George, Edgewater, Maryland

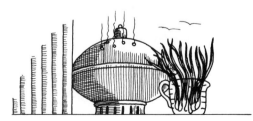

STUFFED KING CRAB LEGS

3 packages (12 ounces each) precooked, frozen king crab legs

1 can (4 ounces) mushroom stems and pieces, drained

2 tablespoons melted butter

2 tablespoons flour

½ teaspoon salt

1 cup milk

½ cup grated cheese

paprika

Thaw frozen crab legs. Remove meat from shells. Remove any cartilage and cut meat into ½-inch pieces. Cook mushrooms in butter for 5 minutes. Blend in flour and salt. Add milk gradually and cook until thick, stirring constantly. Add cheese and crab meat; heat. Fill shells with crab mixture. Sprinkle with paprika. Place stuffed crab legs on a grill, shell side down, about 4 inches from moderately hot coals. Heat for 10 to 12 minutes. Serves 6.

Cooking on the grill is especially appealing for a summer evening. Here's a menu that can be assembled quickly and easily with a little planning—sliced tomatoes, corn-on-the-cob, stuffed king crab legs, and for dessert, have pound cake with a fresh strawberry and banana topping.

Crab Collection

GRILLED KING CRAB LEGS

3 packages (12 ounces each) precooked,
  frozen king crab legs
½ cup butter, melted
2 tablespoons lemon or lime juice
½ teaspoon paprika
melted butter

Thaw frozen crab legs. Combine butter, lemon juice, and paprika. Baste crab meat with sauce. Place crab legs on a grill, flesh side down, about 4 inches from moderately hot coals. Heat for 5 minutes. Turn and baste with sauce. Heat 5 to 7 minutes longer. Serve with melted butter. Serves 6.

The meat is meltingly tender and moist when prepared this way on the grill.

Crab Collection

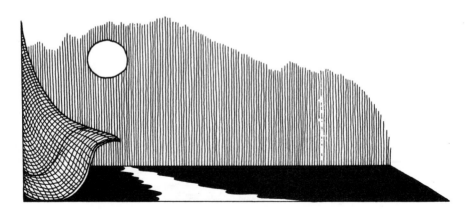

CHOPTANK CRAB FRITTERS

2 cups sliced bamboo shoots
1 cup chopped onion
4 tablespoons soy sauce
1 teaspoon salt
⅛ teaspoon pepper
1 teaspoon ginger
8 eggs, lightly beaten
1 pound crab meat
butter for frying

Combine all ingredients, adding the crab meat last. In a frying pan, heat ½ cup of butter. Drop the fritter mixture by large spoonfuls into the hot butter. Fry to a golden brown, turning once. This makes 8 to 12 servings.

This dish, not as well known as the oyster fritter, is made moist and delicious by the addition of bamboo shoots. Its lightness comes from the beaten eggs, which, when first fried, immediately bind all the ingredients.

Crab Collection

STIR-FRIED DUNGENESS CRAB

2 Dungeness crabs

½ cup water

1 tablespoon cornstarch

2 tablespoons soy sauce

2 tablespoons dry sherry

½ teaspoon sugar

3 tablespoons vegetable oil

2 cloves garlic, crushed

2 slices fresh ginger (¼-inch thick)

1 cup cut-up green onions (1-inch pieces)

With each crab, snap off and discard apron; tear off top shell and save. (Reserve coral and crab fat, if you wish.) Remove spongy gills and soft stomach under the eyes. Remove legs and claws from body. Cut body into 2-inch chunks and crack shell of legs and claws.

In small bowl, combine water, cornstarch, soy sauce, sherry, and sugar.

Heat wok or large saucepot over high heat. Add oil, garlic, and ginger; stir-fry to flavor the oil. Discard garlic and ginger. Add crab and reserved coral, if used. Stir-fry 10 minutes or until shells turn red.

Restir cornstarch mixture; stir into crab along with onions, and toss. Cook until sauce thickens. Transfer to serving platter. Garnish with green onion "brushes," if desired, and top shell of crab. Serves 4.

To really enjoy this family-style dish, you'll need to use your fingers to get the morsels from the crab shells.

Crab Collection

KING CRAB KRUNCH

1 pound king crab meat
1 can (8¾ ounces) crushed pineapple
3 tablespoons butter
½ cup thinly sliced celery
2 tablespoons cornstarch
2 cups chicken broth
½ cup toasted blanched slivered almonds
1 tablespoon lemon juice
1 can (5 ounces) chow mein noodles

Drain pineapple, reserving liquid. Melt butter in a 10-inch fry pan. Add celery, pineapple, and crab meat. Cook over low heat for 5 minutes, stirring frequently. Dissolve cornstarch in pineapple juice. Stir into crab mixture. Add chicken broth gradually and cook until thick, stirring constantly. Add almonds and lemon juice. Serve over noodles. Serves 6.

All types of crab meat can be used interchangeably in these recipes. If you use king crab, either frozen, packed, or fresh, the best meat is taken mostly from the legs.

Crab Collection

CALVERT CRAB NEWBURG

6 tablespoons vegetable oil

3 tablespoons flour

2 cups light cream

⅛ teaspoon nutmeg

dash paprika

1 teaspoon salt

3 tablespoons fresh lemon juice

2 egg yolks

1 pound crab meat

sherry to taste

toast points

parsley

lemon wedges

Heat oil in sauce pan over low heat; stir in the flour and seasoning. After flour has mixed well with the oil, gradually add the cream (which has been heated). Stir constantly until thickened. Beat egg yolks and lemon juice together slightly. Add egg mixture to cream sauce, stirring constantly until egg yolks are cooked. Put crab meat in bottom of casserole. Pour sherry over this and top with the sauce. Brown under broiler. Remove from broiler and serve over toast points, garnish with parsley and lemon wedges. Serves 6.

According to Cy and Pat Liberman, authors of 'The Crab Book', it seems that in New York City around the end of the last century, a gentleman named Wenburg dined frequently at a restaurant famous for its seafood dishes. He became a friend of the restaurateur who, when he created a new seafood concoction, honored one of his star customers by calling it Crab Wenburg. Later the relationship between the two deteriorated, and the restaurateur changed the first syllable of the name to Newburg and deprived Mr. Wenburg of his place in the index of crab-meat cookery.

Crab Collection

KING CRAB NEWBURG

⅓ cup butter
3 tablespoons flour
½ teaspoon salt
½ teaspoon paprika
dash cayenne pepper
1½ cups coffee cream
3 egg yolks
1 pound king crab meat
2 tablespoons sherry
toast points

Melt butter; blend in flour and seasonings. Add cream gradually and cook until thick and smooth, stirring constantly. Stir a little of the hot sauce into egg yolk; add to remaining sauce, stirring constantly. Add crab meat; heat. Remove from heat and slowly stir in sherry. Serve immediately on toast points. Serves 6.

Crab is always king. Serve this Newburg for a refreshing luncheon meal.

Crab Collection

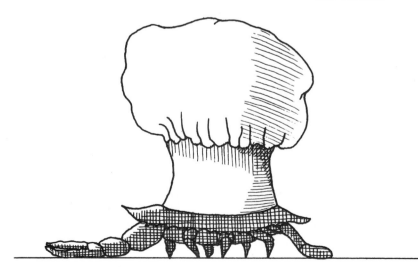

INDEX

APPETIZERS

CRAB CAKES

DEVILED CRAB

INDEX

IMPERIAL CRAB

SALADS

INDEX

SOFT SHELL CRAB

SOUPS

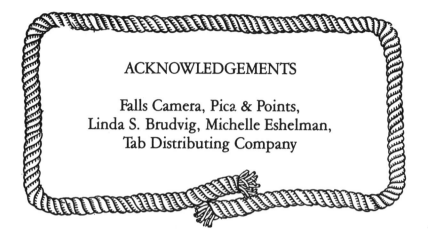

ACKNOWLEDGEMENTS

Falls Camera, Pica & Points,
Linda S. Brudvig, Michelle Eshelman,
Tab Distributing Company

About the Author

"Whitey Schmidt is undoubtedly one of the great characters in the best sense of the word who make the Chesapeake Bay such a special place to live," says Robert L. Perry of the Capital Newspaper. Whitey has crisscrossed the Chesapeake Bay regions for over 25 years to complete the third book in his bay sampler trilogy of seafood dining. It is sure to make a crab enthusiast of any reader.

Bay Country Gift Books

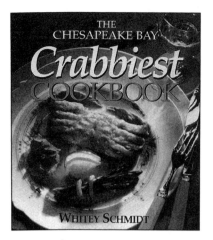

210 flavorful and fun crab recipes

Whitey Schmidt continues his pursuit of delicious crab recipes in *The Chesapeake Bay Crabbiest Cookbook*. You'll find shrimp and crab stew, crab and cheese soufflé, scalloped crab, crab bake and many more—and Whitey's comments and background stories make the recipes as fun to read as they are to cook.

More than 225 photographs capture the unique Chesapeake Bay crab culture, and you'll also find plenty of useful information, such as how to choose the best crabs, the proper way to eat them, and a dictionary of crabbing terms.

8" x 9¼" • hardcover • 248 pages including 8 in full color • 225 photographs • 210 recipes
$29.95 • ISBN: 0-9613008-5-X

Regional recipes from the land of pleasant living

Featuring time-honored traditional dishes, family favorites, and contemporary new creations, this collection of recipes from America's birthplace emerged from the area's diverse cultural heritage and the bounty of seafood and produce available in coastal Maryland and Virginia. Whitey's recipes cover the elegant and the informal, combined with historic anecdotes, relevant commentary, and Marion Warren's superb photography.

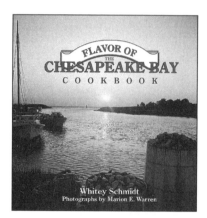

8" x 8½" • paperback • 112 pages • 52 photographs • $13.95 • ISBN: 0-9613008-7-6

TITLE	PRICE	QUANTITY	TOTAL
The Chesapeake Bay Crabbiest Cookbook	$29.95		
Flavor of the Chesapeake Bay Cookbook	$13.95		
The Crab Cookbook	$12.95		
	Subtotal		
	MD Residents add 5% tax		
	Shipping for any qty.		$3.95
	TOTAL		

Name _____

Address _____

City/State/Zip _____

Method of payment: ☐ Check enclosed

☐ Credit card: ___ MC ___ Visa ___ AE

Credit Card No._____

Signature _____ Exp. Date _____

MAIL ORDERS
Marian Hartnett Press
P.O. Box 88, Crisfield, MD 21817
PHONE OR FAX CREDIT CARD ORDERS
888-876-3767